Details in Architecture

Details in Architecture

Creative Detailing

by some of the World's

Leading Architects

First published in Australia in 2002 by
The Images Publishing Group Pty Ltd
ABN 89 059 734 431
6 Bastow Place, Mulgrave, Victoria, 3170, Australia
Telephone: +61 3 9561 5544 Facsimile: +61 3 9561 4860
Email: books@images.com.au
Website: www.imagespublishinggroup.com

National Library of Australia
Cataloguing-in-Publication data

Details in Architecture 4: Creative Detailing by some of the
World's Leading Architects

Includes index.
ISBN: 1 876907 57 6 (v.IV)

1. Architecture – Details. 2. Decoration and ornament,
Architectural

721

Edited by Joe Boschetti
Designed by The Graphic Image Studio Pty Ltd,
Mulgrave, Australia
Film by Mission Productions Limited
Printed by Everbest Printing Co., Ltd.
Printed in Hong Kong/China

IMAGES has included on its website a page for special notices in
relation to this and our other publications. Please visit this site:
www.imagespublishinggroup.com

CONTENTS

CONTENTS

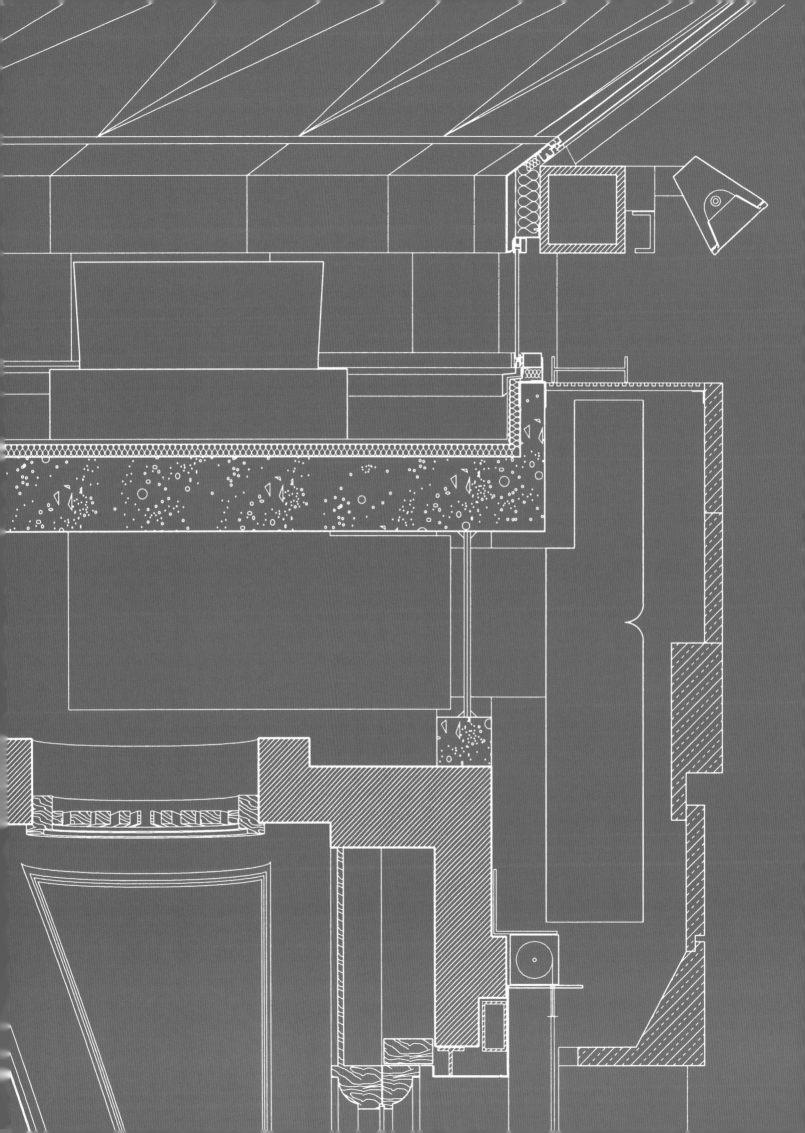

Every work of architecture consists of multiple scales – the scale of site and massing, the scale of exterior and interior spaces, and the scale of detail. A successful building must work to each scale simultaneously.

Historically, the use of hand tools limited the size of building parts, and the dimension of detail was provided by the material used and its joinery. With contemporary techniques of manufacturing and fabrication, the scale of handicraft may not be an inherent standard of measure for this, the smallest, most accessible scale of a building. Instead, we rely on the design of detail – the framing of a window, the profile of a railing, the expression of a connection – to provide this essential human scale.

We find the DNA of the building in its detail, the genetic code particular to time, place and technique. It completes the story and at its best is inevitable. The work in this book celebrates the ability of detail to scale buildings to their occupants, to relate the parts to the whole and, ultimately, to complete the architectural experience.

Mark McInturff
(McInturff Architects, Bethesda, Maryland, USA)

WATER FEATURE
THE CAULDRON, OVERFLOW PARK, HOMEBUSH BAY, NEW SOUTH WALES, AUSTRALIA
Alexander Tzannes Associates, Architecture Urban Design

1

1 Underside of cauldron
2 Site plan
3 Concept design

The Overflow is one of the first examples of the redevelopment of Olympics 2000 venues for post-games use. It is a new public park in the heart of the major facilities at Homebush, between the railway station, the stadium, the dome and the Royal Agricultural Society facilities.

The park design integrates the relocation of the Olympic cauldron as a monument to the medallists and the Sydney 2000 games. The cauldron was rebuilt and significantly modified to allow flames to be lit as required, and provides a fountain and facilities for theatrical lighting.

Adjoining public amenities are integrated through layout and arrangement of landscape, and the use of elements including paving, lighting, general levels, furniture and special landscaped areas.

The design includes a sophisticated employment of art elements to achieve a distinctive environment and to ensure the future relevance of the venue as an interesting place to visit. The artwork by Imants Tillers, in conjunction with the cauldron and landscape design, creates the iconic characteristics of the new park.

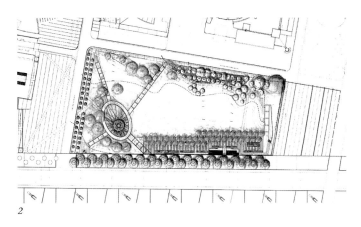

2

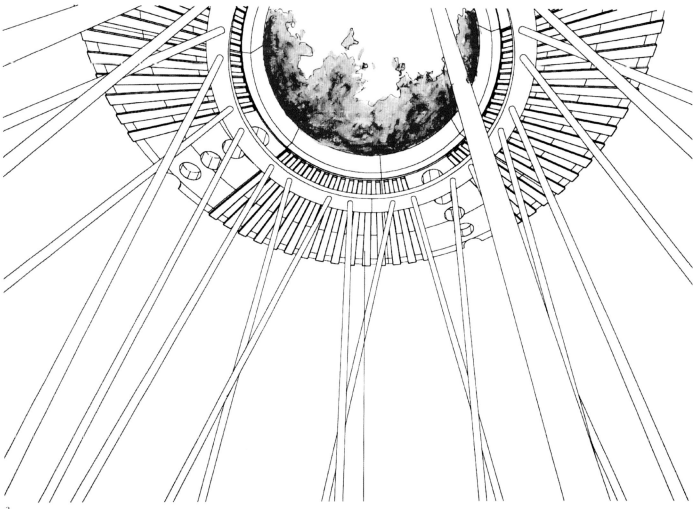

3

The landscape and levels set up a series of interrelated places which are given special significance through the use of paving, art, lighting and text.

Gas and electricity services are designed to operate at various levels of energy usage. The plant facility incorporates recycled water supply for the fountain, with make-up water required primarily for evaporative effects only. Materials are long-life and relatively low in embodied energy. The existing park structures were recycled and major trees were relocated to achieve the landscape concept.

Special considerations in the design are the maintenance arrangements that are simple to service, thus allowing efficient operation. A substantial underground plant houses the services, and keeps them out of public view.

Architecture, landscape architecture, engineering and art all feature to create a unique place of Australian cultural importance.

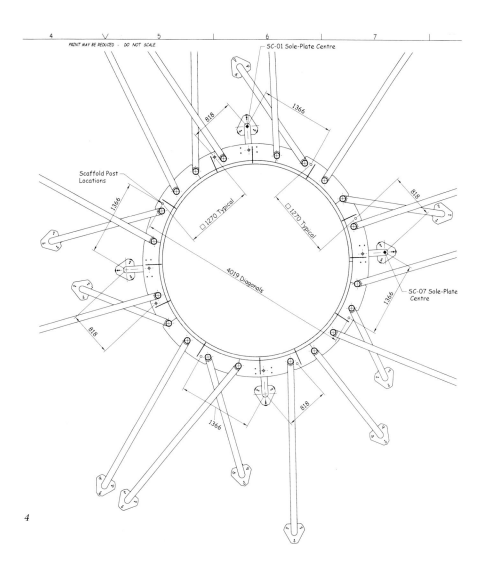

SC-01 Sole-Plate Centre

818

1366

Scaffold Post
Locations

1366

☐ 1270 Typical

☐ 1270 Typical

818

4019 Diagonals

818

SC-07 Sole-Plate
Centre

1366

818

1366

818

4

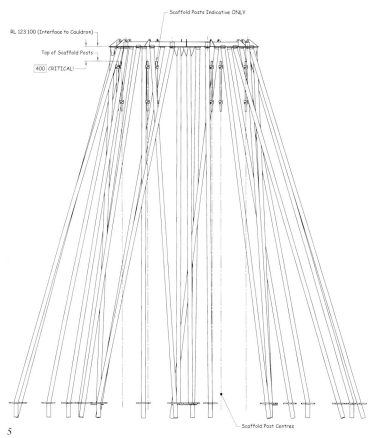

Scaffold Posts Indicative ONLY

RL 123.100 (Interface to Cauldron)

Top of Scaffold Posts

400 CRITICAL!

Scaffold Post Centres

5

4&5   *Scaffold post locations*
Opposite:
     Olympic cauldron

7

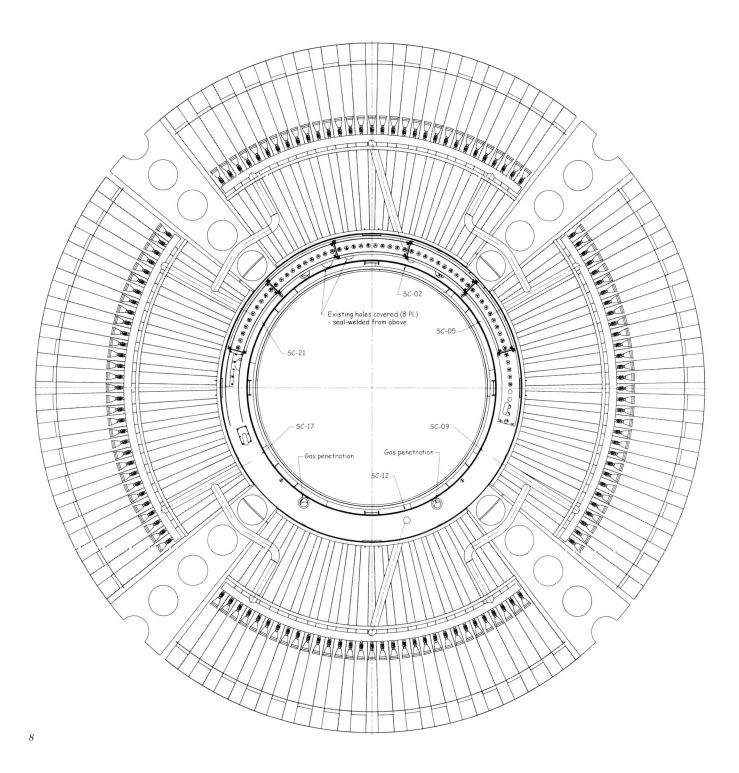

8

15

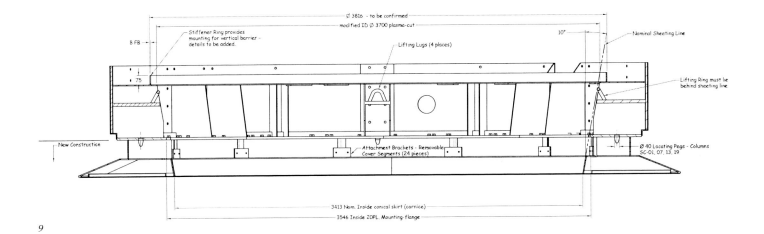

Ø 3816 - to be confirmed

modified ID Ø 3700 plasma-cut

8 FB

Stiffener Ring provides mounting for vertical barrier - details to be added.

10°

Nominal Sheeting Line

Lifting Lugs (4 places)

75

Lifting Ring must lie behind sheeting line

New Construction

Attachment Brackets - Removable Cover Segments (24 pieces)

Ø 40 Locating Pegs - Columns SC-01, 07, 13, 19

3413 Nom. Inside conical skirt (cornice)

3546 Inside 20PL. Mounting-flange

9

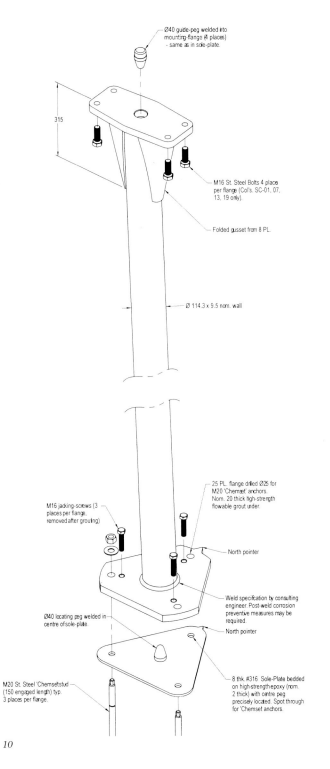

Ø40 guide-peg welded into mounting-flange (4 places) - same as in sole-plate.

315

M16 St. Steel Bolts 4 place per flange (Col's. SC-01, 07, 13, 19 only).

Folded gusset from 8 PL.

Ø 114.3 x 9.5 nom. wall

25 PL. flange drilled Ø25 for M20 'Chemset' anchors. Nom. 20 thick high-strength flowable grout under.

M16 jacking-screws (3 places per flange, removed after grouting)

North pointer

Weld specification by consulting engineer. Post-weld corrosion preventive measures may be required.

Ø40 locating peg welded in centre of sole-plate.

North pointer

M20 St. Steel 'Chemset stud (150 engaged length) typ. 3 places per flange.

8 thk. #316 Sole-Plate bedded on high-strength epoxy (nom. 2 thick) with centre peg precisely located. Spot through for 'Chemset anchors.

10

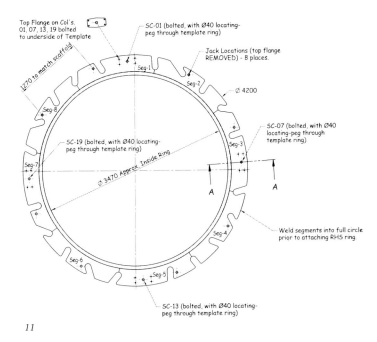

Top Flange on Col's. 01, 07, 13, 19 bolted to underside of Template

SC-01 (bolted, with Ø40 locating-peg through template ring)

Jack Locations (top flange REMOVED) - 8 places.

1270 to match scaffold

Seg-1

Seg-2

Ø 4200

Seg-8

SC-07 (bolted, with Ø40 locating-peg through template ring)

SC-19 (bolted, with Ø40 locating-peg through template ring)

Seg-3

Seg-7

Ø 3470 Approx. Inside Ring

A   A

Weld segments into full circle prior to attaching RHS ring.

Seg-4

Seg-6

Seg-5

SC-13 (bolted, with Ø40 locating-peg through template ring)

11

9   Section
10 Post attachments
11 Template ring weldment
12 Inner shell weldment
13 Gold and silver name plates
Photography: Bart Maiorana
Shop drawings: Design and Survey Neon

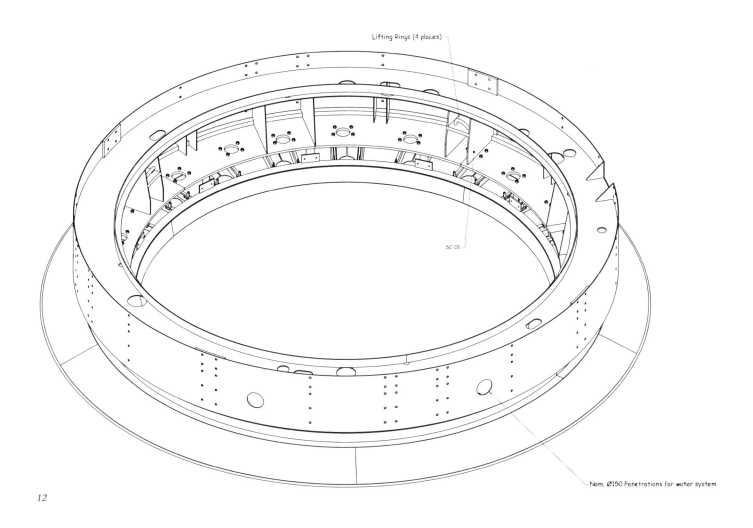

Lifting Rings (4 places)

SC-01

Nom. Ø150 Penetrations for water system

12

13

VAULTED AND DOMED ROOFING SYSTEM
NEW SYDNEY SHOWGROUND, HOMEBUSH BAY, SYDNEY, AUSTRALIA
Ancher/Mortlock/Woolley – Architects

1

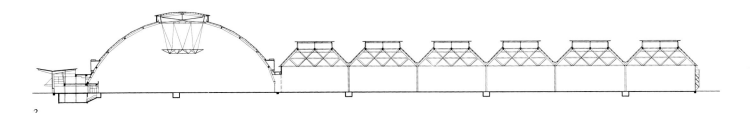

2

A 100-metre dome is the most striking feature of this composition of large building elements housing the exhibition buildings of the Royal Agricultural Society (RAS).

The requirements for the design included a need to accommodate the main exhibition requirements of the RAS in halls with appropriate character, the arrangement of the halls with dimensions to accommodate indoor sporting events for the 2000 Olympics. The hall also had to reflect government policy on ecologically sustainable development, yet be important public buildings of memorable character, scale and

significance as the principle buildings of this component of the Homebush Bay development.

This is the larger and better equipped of the halls and fulfilled the requirement to seat 10,000 volleyball spectators during the 2000 Olympics.

The result incorporates the latest design technology in long-span roofs with vaulting and dome forms made from comparatively short, triangulated sections assembled to act as shell structures. Timber is used for the principal members, with steel remaining the common factor in jointing and tension members, as well as the wall frame and columns.

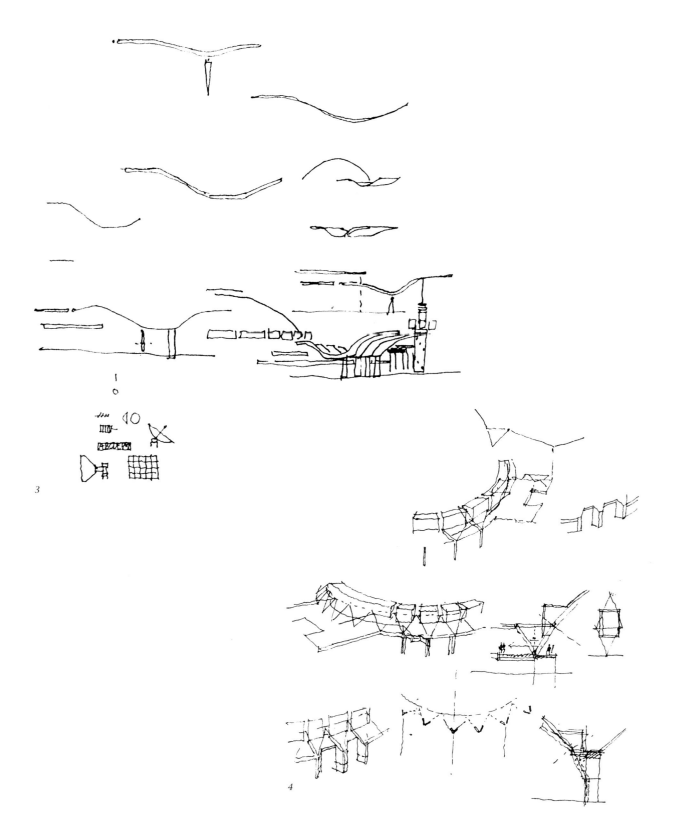

The timber design is a significant response to ESD ambitions for the project. It was found that the cost of time was comparable with steel and enabled the diversification of resources.

The roofs are one of the most significant timber and steel structures in the world since the Lillehammer buildings for the 1994 Winter Olympics. Perhaps more importantly, they will go on more as a permanent expression of a warm and humanistic character, which has been associated for so long with the RAS and the Easter Show.

1   Dome
2   Longitudinal section through Dome Halls 1,2&4
3   Concept sketches for entrance canopy
4   Concept sketches for dome bay windows

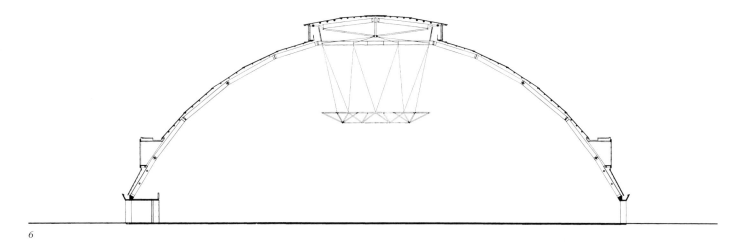

6

7

8

Opposite:
Dome Hall 1 interior
6 Cross section for Dome Hall 1
7 Structure and ventilating louvres of monitor roof over dome
8 Erection process starts with top section assembled on floor then lifted one ring at a time
9 Detail section of monitor roof to Dome Hall 1

The administration building incorporates the formal entrance to the main dome Exhibition Hall and the entrance to the showground from the new railway station. The building provides an urban-scale street edge to a railway square, turning to a similar colonnade edge to the pedestrian concourse leading into the centre of the showground. On this corner there are mobile turnstiles and ticketing, festive signs and flags.

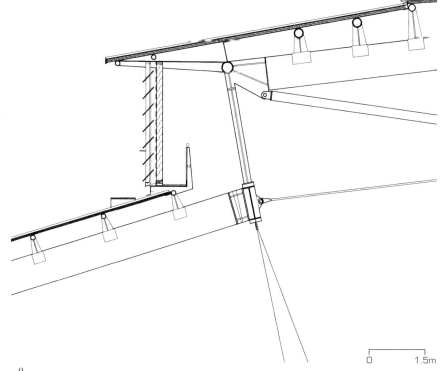

9

0   1.5m

11

Opposite:
Bay windows of the dome
11 *Close up of bay windows in Dome Hall 1*
12 *Section through bay windows, ring beam gutter and colonnade to Dome Hall 1*

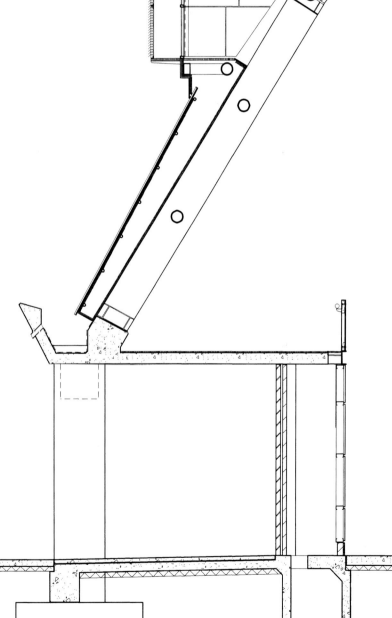

A circular tower presents giant television screens, signs, electronic messages and flags, which provide a strong marker for this corner of the showground. The tower can also take communication antennae and dishes and may have a public lookout, if desired.

The main canopy also uses the large laminated timber sections as columns and cantilevers. Externally, the timber is sheathed in copper.

12

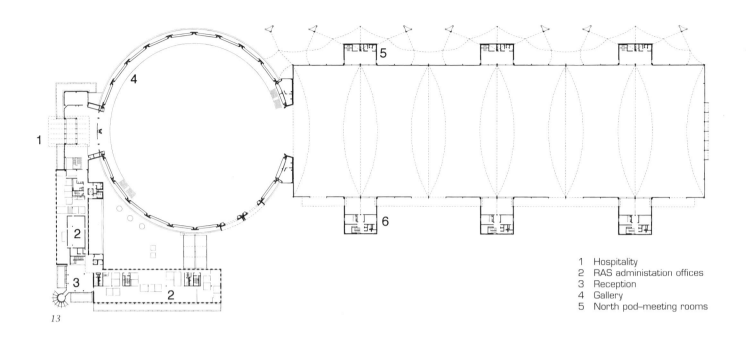

1 Hospitality
2 RAS administration offices
3 Reception
4 Gallery
5 North pod—meeting rooms

13

14

15

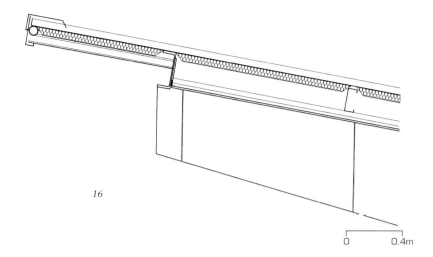

16

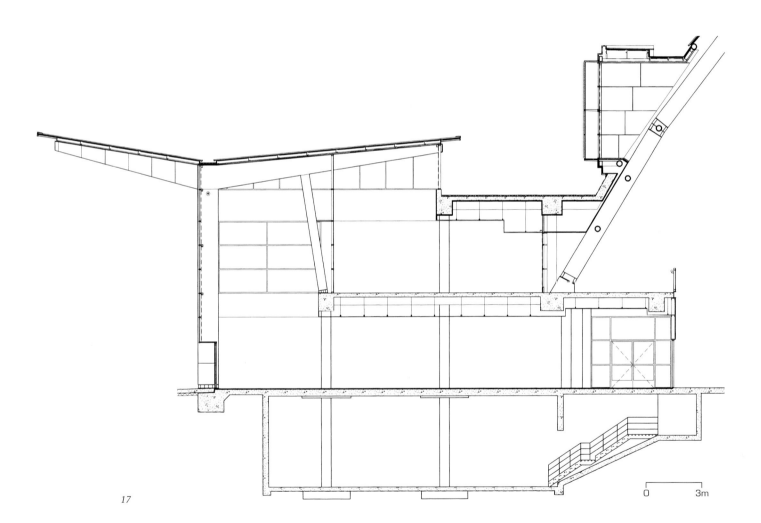

17

0   0.4m

0   3m

13 Level-one floor plan
14 Entrance canopy, laminated timber
    structure clad externally with copper
15 Entrance canopy and foyer elevation
16 Detail section of entrance canopy, eaves
    and copper-clad beam
17 Section through entrance canopy, entry
    hall and mezzanine hospitality areas to
    Dome Hall 1

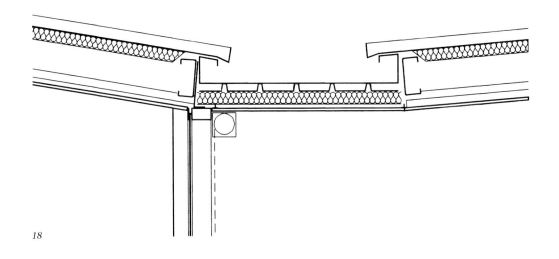

18

19

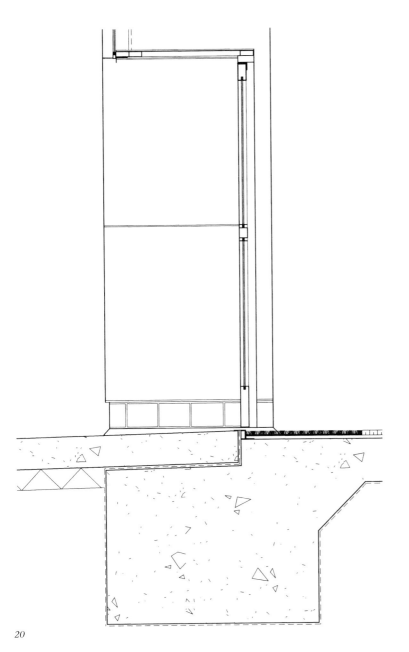

18   *Detail section of box gutter and sun control blinds to entrance canopy*
19   *Administration building and main entrance*
20   *Detail section through entrance canopy doors and copper-clad blade columns*
21   *Entry hall timber structure*
Photography: Patrick Bingham-Hall (1,5,10,11,15,19); Garry Wallace (7,8,16,21)
Concept sketches: Ken Woolley

20

21

NAVE, TRANSEPT, STEEPLE, BAPTISTRY AND CHANCEL
NOTRE DAME DE L'ARCHE D'ALLIANCE, PARIS, FRANCE
Architecture Studio

1

2

3

This church in the centre of Paris symbolises the Ark of the Covenant.

Its cubical shape, reflecting both perfection and simplicity, is incorporated into a metallic grid that surrounds the building. The grid represents the transition between the outside world and the sanctuary of the church.

Inside, the short nave leads to the apse and crosses the equally proportioned transept, accentuating both the coherence and vertical nature of the interior.

The transept separates the nave and the apse. Its cross opens in a cubic vault exposed to the light with a conical clerestory that faces the altar.

The steeple is an empty 48-metre-high silo, which is a symbolic elevation of the church. Unlike a closed, solid tower, it is easy to imagine the wind blowing through its structure.

The baptistery differs from early church baptisteries, which were separate from the church. While it is still a sacred monument dedicated to the rite of Christian initiation, it is positioned

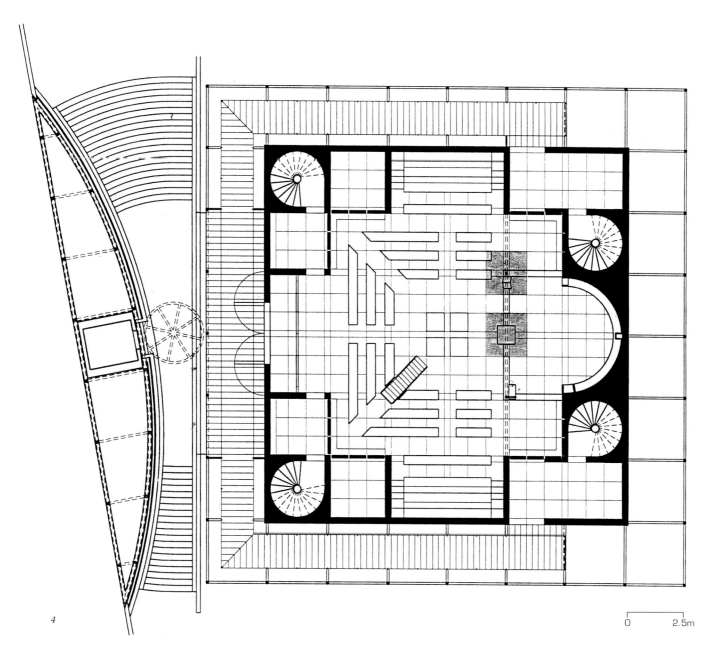

4

0   2.5m

beneath the Ark – under the church. It is a stone
monolith in a white crypt, with a vertical light
crossing the upper level, and marked by a crucifix.

The chancel is shaped like a slightly inclined
cylinder, and the façade is parabolic. It is in the
shape of a Greek cross with equal branches, and
is an orientation point in the church.

One enters the building through big wooden
doors, which are reminiscent of the heavy panels
used in traditional church structures.

1   Steeple
2   Nave
3   Baptistery
4   Ambo

5

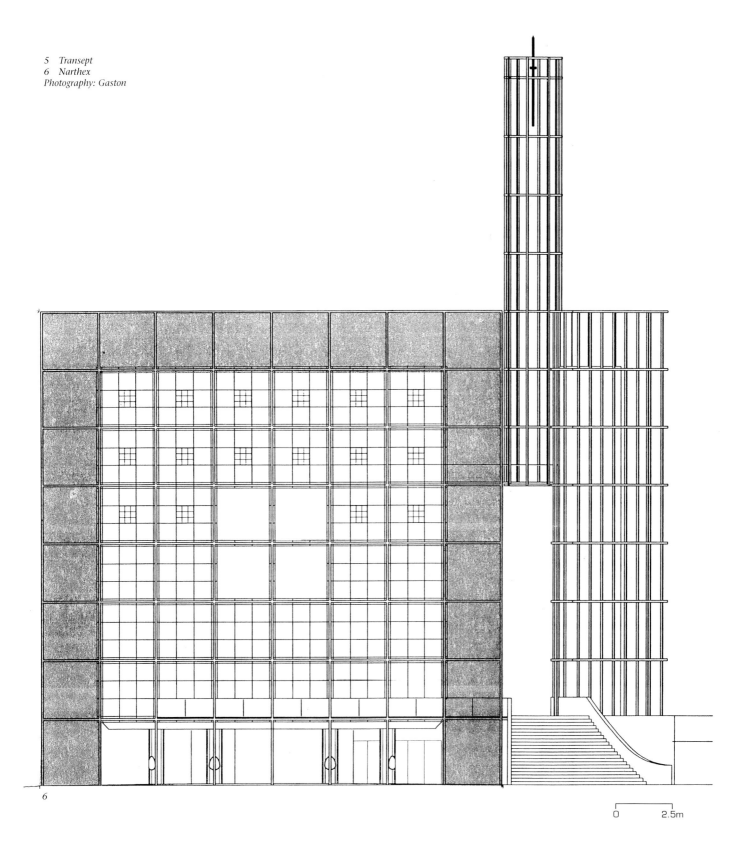

6

0   2.5m

ROOF, HONEYCOMB CEILING, CRUCIFORM PILLARS AND HEMICYCLE

EUROPEAN PARLIAMENT HOUSE, STRASBOURG, FRANCE
Architecture Studio

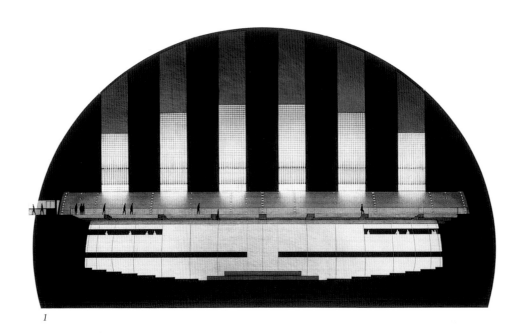

1

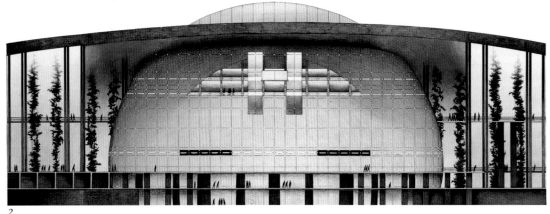

2

The design mandate for the European Parliament was to express the history and culture of Europe, while simultaneously representing our era and the democratic institution that supports it.

The structure is representative of the foundations of Western civilisation – both classicism and baroque. The passage from the central geometric structure (Galileo) to the anamorphosis (Borromini), the ellipse (Kepler, Gongora), an unstable period in geometry, representing the passage from a central power to democracy.

The European Parliament will be recognised, directly or via the transmission of images, and be autonomous.

It takes into account the broad environmental morphology of Europe, as well as the two notions of 'city' and Europe. While an expression of antimony, they remain connected and complementary.

This building has, simultaneously, the strength of power, and the openness of democracy.

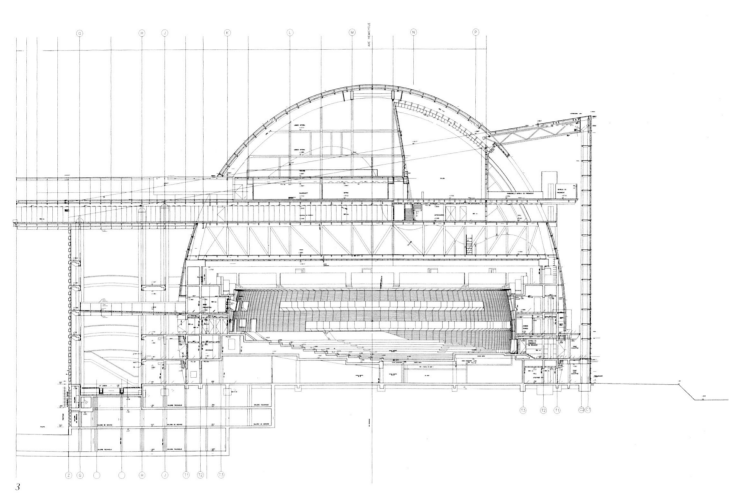

3

4

1   Cross-section of the hemicycle
2   Façade elevation
3   Detail section of hemicycle
4   Roof detail
Photography: G. Fessy

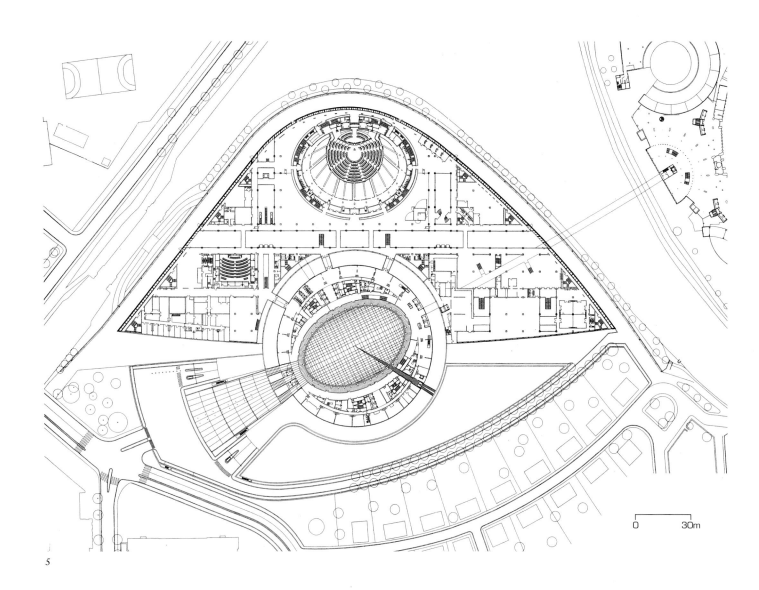

5

5 Plan
6 Ceiling detail: complex honeycomb
   structure, delivering lighting and acoustics
7 Cafeteria
Photography: R. Rothan (6); G. Fessy (7)

6

7

GLASS CURTAINWALL
Royal Military Academy Conference Centre, Brussels, Belgium
ASSAR (pilot) – Teams

1

1 General view
2 Detail showing roof structure and façade brise-soleil
3 Main entrance facing garden plaza

The 2,700-square-metre conference centre is the most recent addition to the Royal Military Academy. It comprises a 300-seat auditorium and a 50-seat symposium room with state-of-the-art equipment and recording rooms.

The glass façade allows natural light to enter the main auditorium, which is controlled by automated louvres when necessary. The use of a spider-type arm system generates a sense of lightness. The façade structure is made of steel with acoustic windows. The glass façades are equipped with steel 'bridges' to aid cleaning.

Two English courtyards, made from Belgian natural stone, were built along the lateral to allow natural light into the basement.

The conference centre is covered by a vaulted metal roof. Inside, basic colours such as white, grey and black are found, and material such as wood, steel and granite have been used.

The Royal Military Academy Conference Centre can also be used by people and organisations that do not belong to the army. A glass 'inside' entrance faces the garden plaza while a second

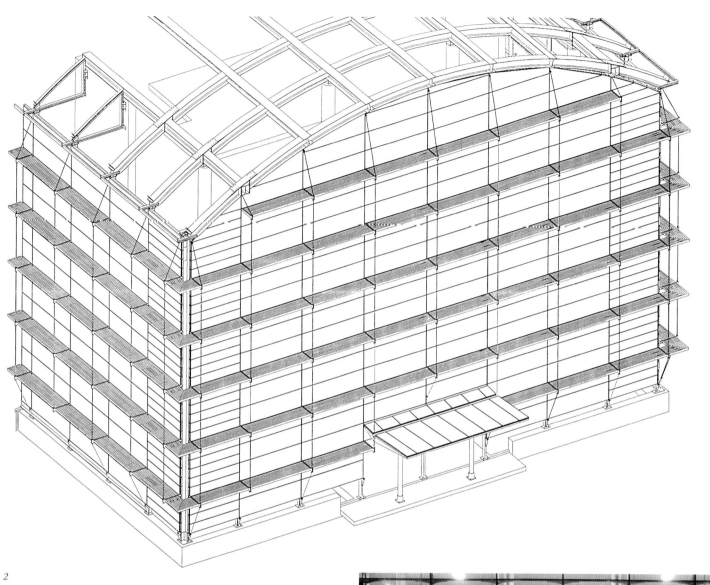

2

'outside' entrance has been designed facing the street. This entrance is made of bricks, architectonic prefabricated concrete and bluestone to comply with the more classic ambiance of the buildings facing Leonardo da Vinci Street.

3

4

5

4 Façade details showing brise-soleil made
   of steel 'bridges' in order to ease cleaning
5 Inside view of glass wall as seen from
   vertical circulation
6 Main entrance details showing brise-soleil
   made of steel 'bridges' and canopy
7 Detail showing roof structure and façade
   brise-soleil
Photography: Marc Detiffe

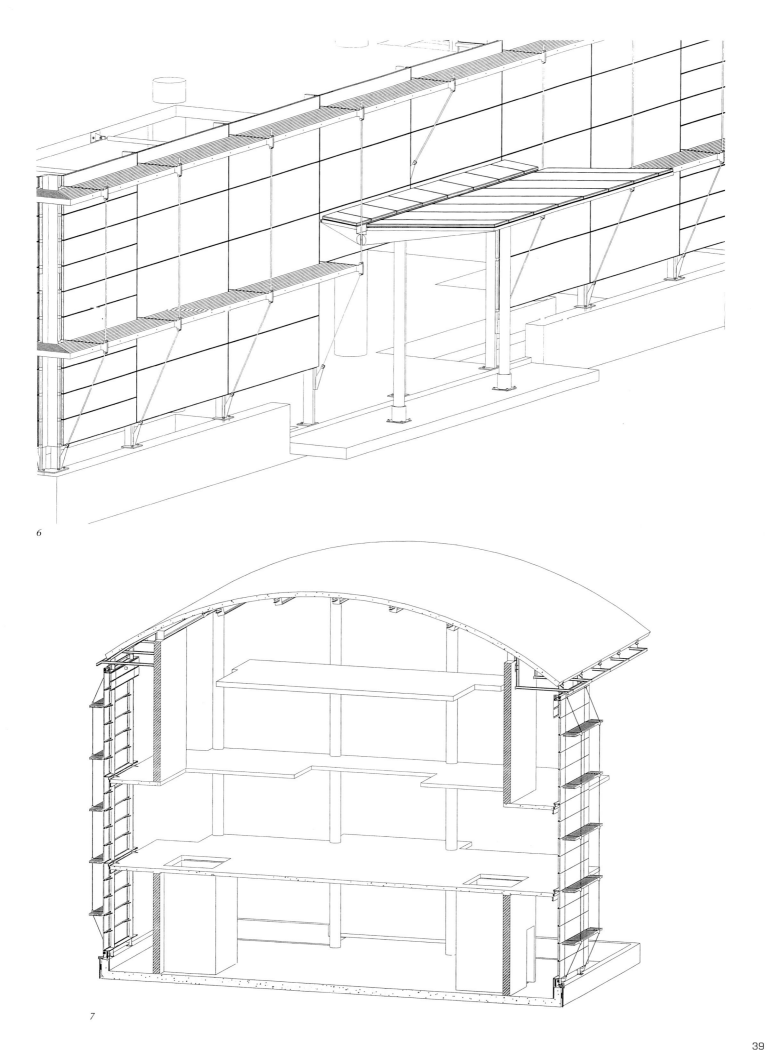

6

7

LEAFED GLAZING
SPA BAD ELSTER, BAD ELSTER, GERMANY
Behnisch & Partner

2

1

Albert Spa, Bad Elster Spa, is one of Germany's oldest mud baths. The complex comprises a collection of buildings dating from 1856 and 1912, including a renovation from 1909–10, which has a strong Jugendstil influence.

The new development includes several new pools, mostly located in a new central bathing hall. The facilities also include an information pavilion and a new therapy building for massage and mud treatments.

The building that accommodates the spa is traditionally beautiful and attractive. Any massing of the interior courtyard had to be avoided and accommodate a full view of the sky and the surrounding wooded hills.

The covering incorporates transparent materials. Similarly, the enclosing walls are also transparent so that the necessary partition between the inside and outside is hardly perceived.

The new building deliberately contrasts with the old buildings. The clear, sober shape of the state-of-the-art building technologies allows transparency, light structures and light colours to create a serene and pleasant atmosphere, turning the hall into an element of the landscape of the interior courtyard.

3

The façade and the roof consist of double-leafed glazed elements with a distance of 1 metre between the leafs. Both leafs are transom-mullion constructions with pressure fixtures. The air between the leafs operate in winter as an insulating buffer, and condensation is avoided with a permanent air flow through the corridor, and thermal energy is generated between the leafs.

At night and when the temperature drops below 0 degrees Celsius, the glazing is closed to create an air buffer to shield from heat loss. Exhaust air is conducted between the two leafs of the northern façade, where a separate duct is created by installing a glass membrane. Visible ducts are not necessary. The duct is accessible for easy cleaning.

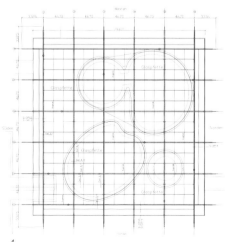

4

1 Old forms contrast with new
2 Leafed glazing filters light and colour onto neutral surfaces
3 Louvres regulate light and temperature for comfort of bathers
4 Steel-grid structure supports louvre system above pools

5 Glass is white frit-printed on upper sides
   (facing sky) and colour frit-printed on
   lower sides (facing interior)
6 Section through double façade
7 Section through horizontal louvre system
   showing operations
Photography: Christian Kandzia

5

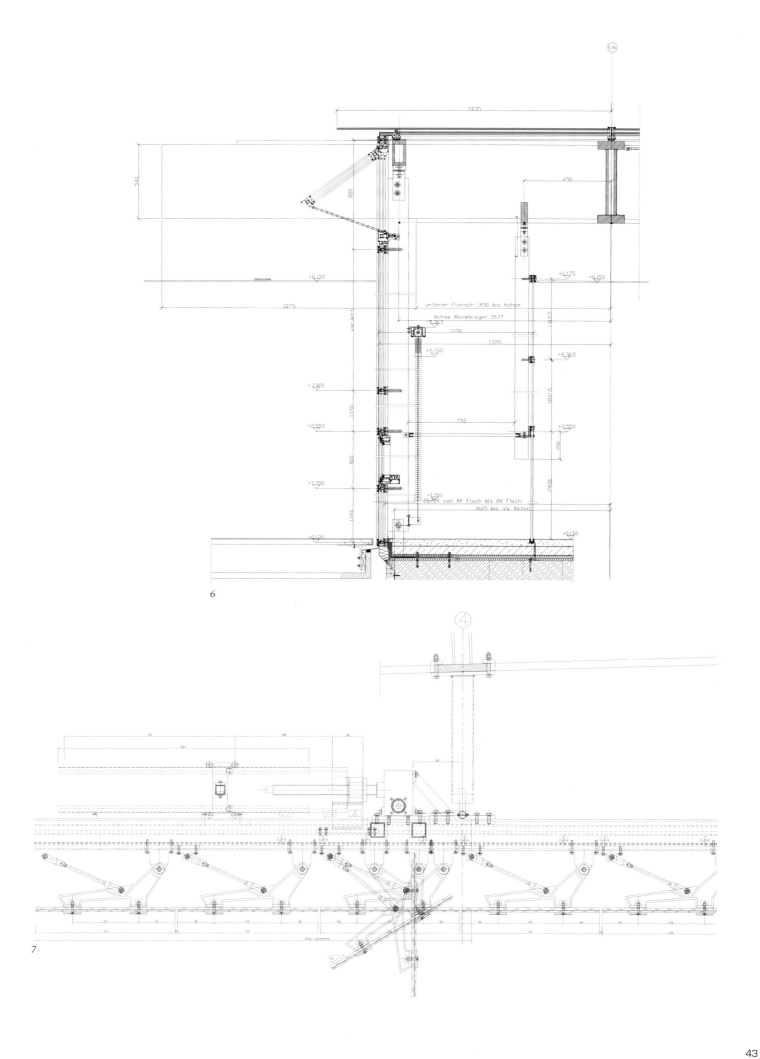

6

7

CARVED WALLS
LAGUNA BEACH RESORT, PHUKET, THAILAND
Belt Collins

1

Based on the ancient Khmer stone carvings at the Angkor Temple Complex in Cambodia, Belt Collins incorporated a contemporary interpretation of the Elephant Wall and Naga Warrior sculptures of the temple complex into the design of the swimming pool and water features at the Laguna Beach Resort project in Phuket.

The sculptures were constructed out of a reinforced concrete structure. A team of local craftspeople were responsible for hand carving the finished artwork. Careful attention was given to the colouring of the surfaces to ensure that the final appearance of the sculptures closely matched the colour of the original weathered beige sandstone sculptures.

Belt Collins' team of designers made numerous study visits to Angkor during the design and construction of the project to ensure details such as the form, texture and colour of the sculptures were as authentic as possible.

The elephant sculpture wall is a series of 3.5-metre-high walls that enclose the main swimming pool area of the resort. Combined with lush

2

3

4

plantings and planter areas built into the walls for climbing plants, the final effect of the feature walls is dramatic.

The Naga Warrior sculptures are a double row of 28 1.5-metre-high sculptures lining one of the swim-through pool areas, which links the main pool to one of the smaller fun pools. The combination of cascading water, sunken pool seats, lush planting and up-lighting makes this one of the most popular and dramatic areas of the resort.

1 Perspective sketch of Naga Warrior sculpture
2 Elevation sketch of Elephant Wall sculpture
3 Finished Naga Warrior sculpture
4 Finished Elephant Wall sculpture
Photography: courtesy Belt Collins

HELIPORT
ATTILIO TINELLI, BROOKLIN NOVO, SÃO PAULO, BRAZIL
Carlos Bratke Ateliê de Arquitetura

1

2

This heliport was an afterthought. The architect was instructed to include it on the top of the Attilio Tinelli building when the building was nearing the final phase of its construction.

Rather than trying to mimic the overall design, the heliport represents a different design point from the rest of the building.

The design represents a play of geometric shapes, similar to a game with boxes. Visible in the design is both a door that is opening and a cube that is placed inside another cube.

1   Roof showing helipad
2   Heliport from above
3   View from front showing play of cube forms
4   Front elevation
5   Section of metallic structure
Photography: José Moscardi Jr

3

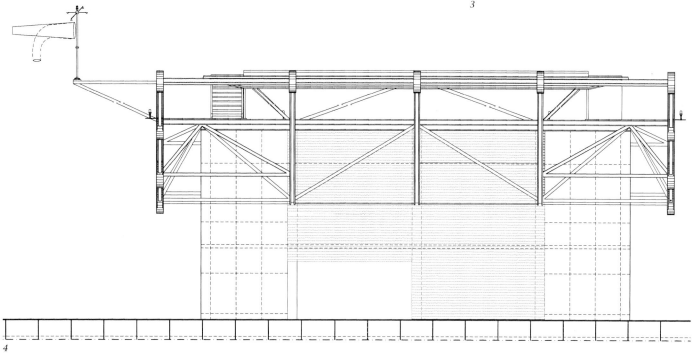

4

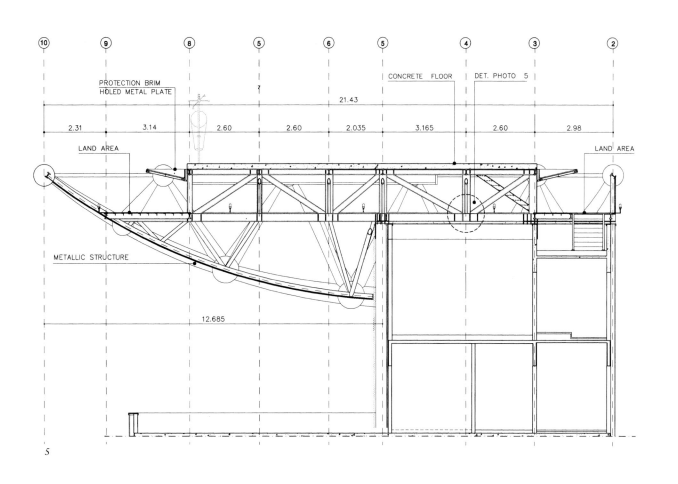

PROTECTION BRIM
HOLED METAL PLATE

CONCRETE FLOOR   DET. PHOTO 5

21.43

2.31   3.14   2.60   2.60   2.035   3.165   2.60   2.98

LAND AREA   LAND AREA

METALLIC STRUCTURE

12.685

5

GRANITE PIER, FENCE AND GATE
BOSTON LDS TEMPLE PROJECT, BELMONT, MASSACHUSETTS, USA
Carol R. Johnson Associates, Inc.

1

2

Located atop the second highest hill in the Boston metropolitan area, the Boston Massachusetts Temple of The Church of Jesus Christ of Latter-day Saints serves church members throughout eastern New England. This picturesque 2.8-hectare site, marked by more than 1.2 hectares of surface rock and ledge outcroppings, drops over 24.4 metres from north to south.

The landscape design philosophy focused on tailoring the site program elements to the constraints of the site while preserving its natural views and qualities. The site's unique topography and dramatic exposed rock surfaces required the

blasting and removal of more than 50,300 cubic metres of rock to fit the 9750 square-metre temple site and related gardens, parking and walks onto two developed hectares. A granite-veneer retaining wall, ranging in height from 4.6 to 9.2 metres, was constructed to achieve the required accessible grades and separated the developed landscape from the remaining two wooded acres on which mature trees were preserved.

Temple patrons are invited to the temple entrance by the Great Lawn, which is flanked by graceful curved granite walls that extend from the building's central entrance.

1　Illustrative site plan (not to scale)
2　Temple, great lawn and perimeter fencing
3&5　Granite veneer retaining wall and plantings
4　Gate pier

3

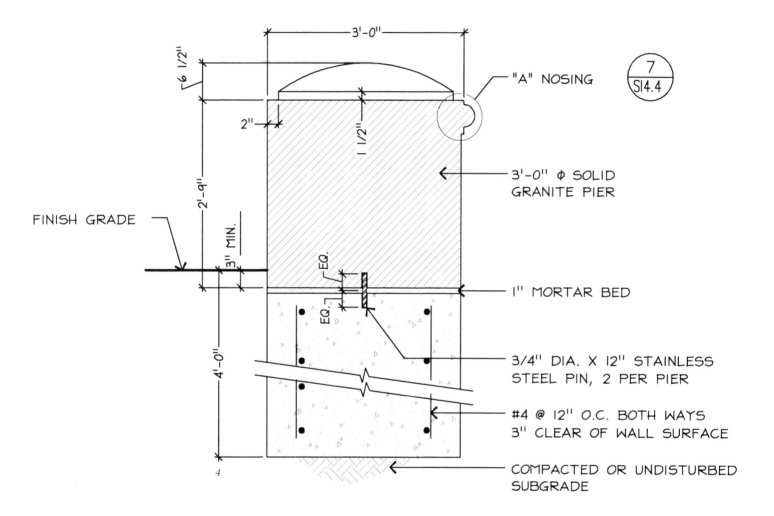

3'-0"

6 1/2"

"A" NOSING

⑦
S14.4

2"

1 1/2"

FINISH GRADE

2'-9"

3" MIN.

3'-0" Φ SOLID
GRANITE PIER

EQ.

EQ.

1" MORTAR BED

4'-0"

3/4" DIA. X 12" STAINLESS
STEEL PIN, 2 PER PIER

#4 @ 12" O.C. BOTH WAYS
3" CLEAR OF WALL SURFACE

4

COMPACTED OR UNDISTURBED
SUBGRADE

Additional site features include custom ornamental iron entry gates and perimeter fencing. A variety of gardens located throughout the developed site provide views to the rich New England landscape in the distance, as well as quiet places of contemplation for use by personal and small group gatherings.

5

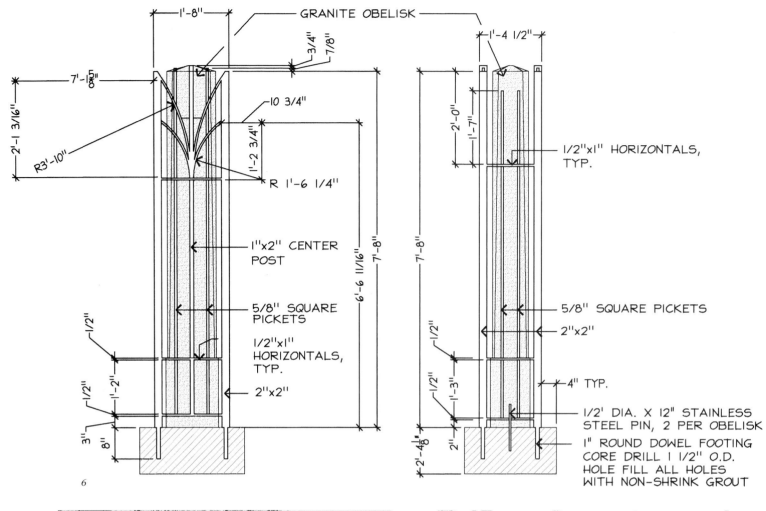

GRANITE OBELISK

1'-8"

3/4"
7/8"

7'-1½"

2'-1 3/16"

R3'-10"

10 3/4"

1'-2 3/4"

R 1'-6 1/4"

1"x2" CENTER POST

5/8" SQUARE PICKETS

1/2"x1" HORIZONTALS, TYP.

2"x2"

1/2"

1/2"
1'-2"

3"
8"

6'-6 11/16"

7'-8"

6

1'-4 1/2"

2'-0"

1'-7"

1/2"x1" HORIZONTALS, TYP.

7'-8"

5/8" SQUARE PICKETS

2"x2"

1/2"

1/2"
1'-3"

2"

4" TYP.

1/2' DIA. X 12" STAINLESS STEEL PIN, 2 PER OBELISK

1" ROUND DOWEL FOOTING CORE DRILL 1 1/2" O.D. HOLE FILL ALL HOLES WITH NON-SHRINK GROUT

2'-4⅛"

7

8

6 *Gate pier*
7 *Great lawn and granite site walls at temple entrance*
8 *Enclosed granite obelisk at entry gate pier*
9 *Section of ovalwall*
10 *Granite veneer retaining wall and plantings*
Photography: Jerry Brown and Jerry Howard

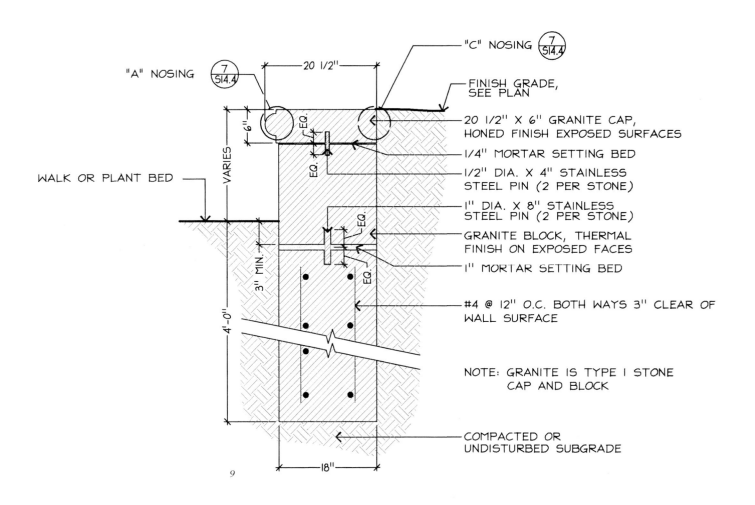

"A" NOSING ⑦/514.4

"C" NOSING ⑦/514.4

20 1/2"

6"

VARIES

EQ.

WALK OR PLANT BED

EQ.

EQ.

3" MIN.

4'-0"

18"

9

FINISH GRADE, SEE PLAN

20 1/2" X 6" GRANITE CAP, HONED FINISH EXPOSED SURFACES

1/4" MORTAR SETTING BED

1/2" DIA. X 4" STAINLESS STEEL PIN (2 PER STONE)

1" DIA. X 8" STAINLESS STEEL PIN (2 PER STONE)

GRANITE BLOCK, THERMAL FINISH ON EXPOSED FACES

1" MORTAR SETTING BED

#4 @ 12" O.C. BOTH WAYS 3" CLEAR OF WALL SURFACE

NOTE: GRANITE IS TYPE I STONE CAP AND BLOCK

COMPACTED OR UNDISTURBED SUBGRADE

10

STAIR AND SERVER ROOM

INNOVENTRY, SAN FRANCISCO, CALIFORNIA, USA

Cass Calder Smith Architecture

1

Innoventry is a commercial tenant improvement of an 18,228-square-metre area for a high-tech financial services firm located in San Francisco. The firm wanted a showcase office for its San Francisco headquarters, which would house a mix of corporate financial offices, technology developers and administration.

The site is a recently renovated four-storey structure with garage located in a former dry-dock facility. Set up for multi-tenancy, it had a relatively small floor plate not easily suited to a single tenant.

The clients wanted to foster communication between floors and departments, as well as to allow for a flexible open office environment that would allow for growth and expansion. The solution was to connect the floors through a central circulation spine in the form of a stair. This penetrated the various floors on one axis, and stacked program around that axis-spine on all of the floors.

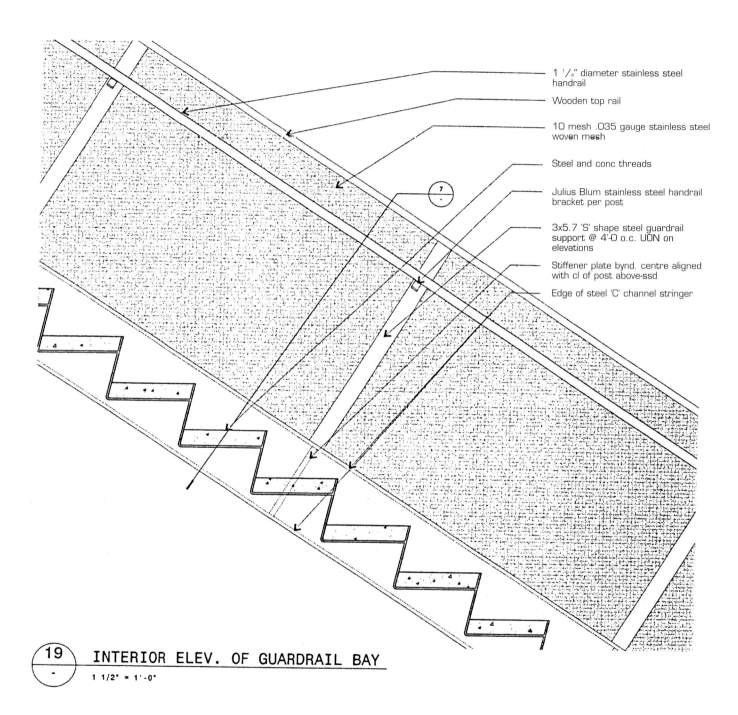

1 Internal linking stair with break area beyond
2 Interior elevation of guardrail bay

1 ¹/₄" diameter stainless steel handrail

Wooden top rail

10 mesh .035 gauge stainless steel woven mesh

Steel and conc threads

Julius Blum stainless steel handrail bracket per post

3x5.7 'S' shape steel guardrail support @ 4'-0 o.c. UON on elevations

Stiffener plate bynd. centre aligned with cl of post above-ssd

Edge of steel 'C' channel stringer

⟨19⟩ INTERIOR ELEV. OF GUARDRAIL BAY
  -
      1 1/2" = 1'-0"

2

Opposite:
Detail of stair at fourth floor with
stainless mesh wrap and conference room
beyond
4   *Rendering of central stair*
5   *Detail at handrail*

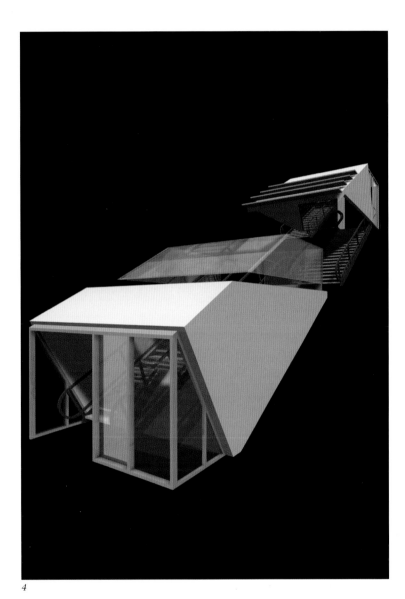

4

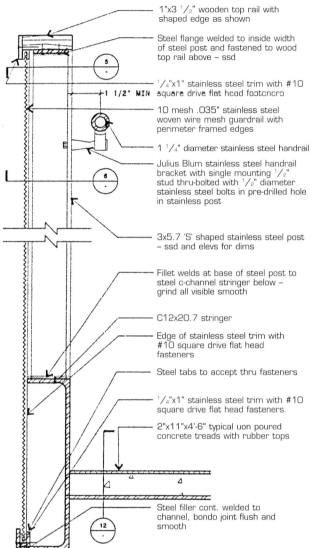

1"x3 ¹/₂" wooden top rail with shaped edge as shown

Steel flange welded to inside width of steel post and fastened to wood top rail above – ssd

¹/₄"x1" stainless steel trim with #10 square drive flat head fasteners

10 mesh .035" stainless steel woven wire mesh guardrail with perimeter framed edges

1 ¹/₄" diameter stainless steel handrail

Julius Blum stainless steel handrail bracket with single mounting ¹/₂" stud thru-bolted with ¹/₂" diameter stainless steel bolts in pre-drilled hole in stainless post

3x5.7 'S' shaped stainless steel post – ssd and elevs for dims

Fillet welds at base of steel post to steel c-channel stringer below – grind all visible smooth

C12x20.7 stringer

Edge of stainless steel trim with #10 square drive flat head fasteners

Steel tabs to accept thru fasteners

¹/₄"x1" stainless steel trim with #10 square drive flat head fasteners

2"x11"x4'-6" typical uon poured concrete treads with rubber tops

Steel filler cont. welded to channel, bondo joint flush and smooth

1 1/2" MIN

5

The top floor was reserved for conferencing and meeting spaces, concentrating major facilities such as break rooms, conferencing and arterial support around the 'spine'. It stretched from the ground-floor lobby to the uppermost floor in a direct line, with support located centrally around it.

In cases such as the server room, program stretched in a violation of the perimeter enclosure and cantilevered over the main lobby in order to maintain its relationship to the spine.

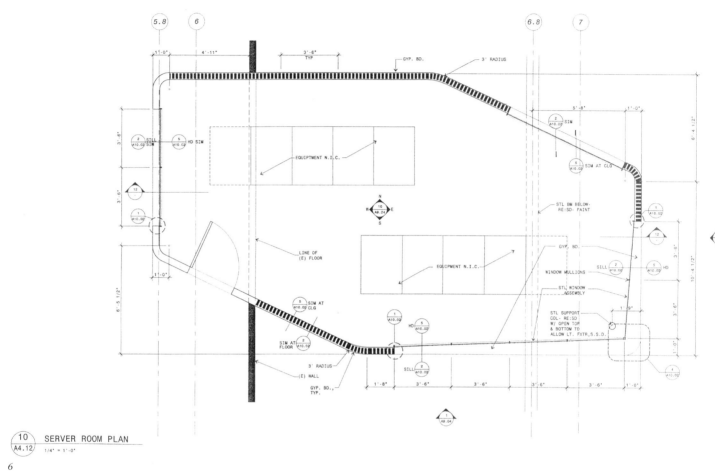

5.8	6	

11'-0" 4'-11" 3'-6" TYP GYP. BD. 3' RADIUS

6.8 7

3'-6"
SILL SIM   HD SIM

5'-8" 1'-0"

SIM

SIM AT CLG

6'-4 1/2"

3'-6"

EQUIPTMENT N.I.C.

STL BM BELOW-
RE:SD- PAINT

11'-0"

LINE OF
(E) FLOOR

EQUIPMENT N.I.C.

GYP. BD.

WINDOW MULLIONS

SILL   HD

3'-6"

STL WINDOW
ASSEMBLY

3'-4 1/2"

6'-5 1/2"

SIM AT
CLG

STL SUPPORT
COL- RE:SD
W/ OPEN TOP
& BOTTOM TO
ALLOW LT. FXTR,S.S.D.

3'-6"

SIM AT
FLOOR

HD

1'-9"

1'-0"

3' RADIUS

(E) WALL

GYP. BD.,
TYP.

SILL

1'-8" 3'-6" 3'-6" 3'-6" 3'-6" 1'-0"

10 SERVER ROOM PLAN
A4.12   1/4" = 1'-0"

6

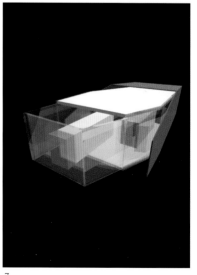

6   Plan at server room
7   Server room study
Opposite:
   *Above main lobby/entrance with server
   room above*

7

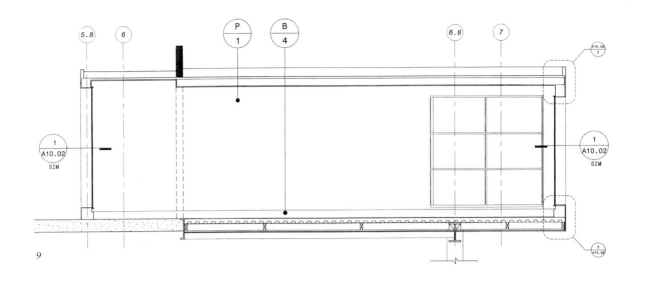

9

9   Server room section
10 Main reception with custom reception
    desk and server room above
Opposite:
    Above main lobby/entrance with server
    room above
Photography: Michael O'Callahan

10

TWIN-SKIN CLADDING
POLYMER ENGINEERING CENTRE, KANGAN BATMAN TAFE, BROADMEADOWS, VICTORIA, AUSTRALIA
Cox Sanderson Ness

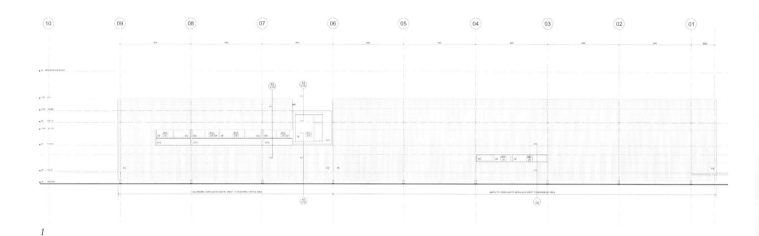

1

2

1   *West elevation*
2   *Polymer façade at night*
3   *TAFE at dusk*
4   *Skin and structure analysis*

The Polymer Engineering Centre is a simulated plastics manufacturing plant, incorporating thermoplastic processing and recycling techniques, with supporting laboratory, meeting and multimedia/multi-use spaces for staff and teaching.

The building references its use – the technique of extrusion through a single section used in some plastics manufacturers is magnified to the scale of the building's section. This shape reappears, not only in the details of windows and decorative panels, but as the structural section repeated along the 80-metre length of the building.

The white tube-like form dominates the sloping site and is visible from far below the campus. At the scale of a two-storey building, and in the context of surfaces comprised largely of plastics, the building evokes a futuristic fantasy of lightness and plasticity, as well as the ephemeral.

The outer twin-skin cladding allows for temperature control, and adds a positive environmental contribution to the project. This provides a lightweight solution to thermal stacking, reducing thermal bridging and direct heat transmittance.

3

The result is increased energy efficiency and reduced lifecycle costs in both winter and summer.

The two layers of plastic catch air which is forced through to cool the building in summer, but trapped and heated by the sun to warm the building in winter.

The transparency of the material also allows natural light into the workshop, resulting in an active space that students love working in.

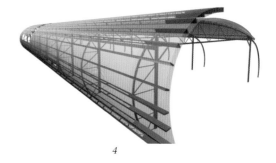

4

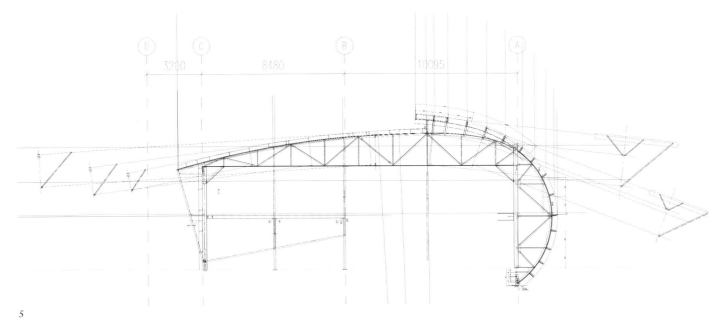

5

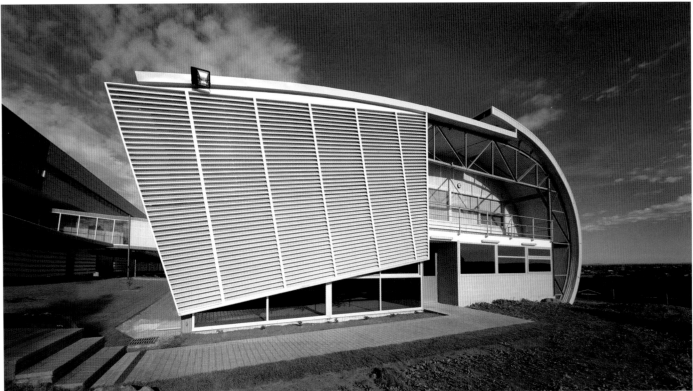

6

5   Section
6   Northeast elevation
7   Cladding detail
8   South elevation
Photography: Dianna Snape

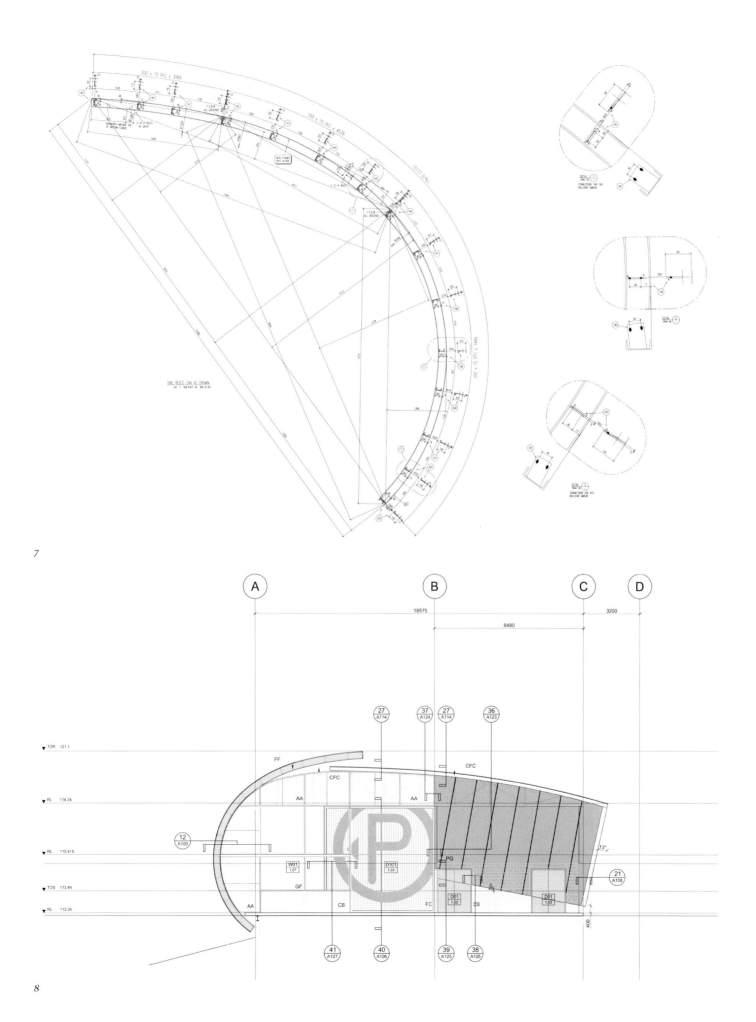

7

8

THREE-DIMENSIONAL ROOF
NATIONAL WINE CENTRE, ADELAIDE, SOUTH AUSTRALIA, AUSTRALIA
Cox Grieve

1

1 *Busby Hall*
2 *Three-dimensional roof*
3 *Cross section*

Australia's National Wine Centre takes its lead from the Australian Wine Industry in using a broad range of technologies from the traditional to the state-of-art scientific approach. This is best embodied in the diagrid roof to the Busby Hall, that uses almost domestic-scale timber elements engineered into a shell structure with pre-stressed stainless steel cables.

The 600-square-metre Busby Hall with a roof span of 13 metres is curved in plan with the roof curved in section. The aim was to develop a structure using '4 by 2s', a structure that relies on simple, easily obtained Hoop Pine sections, manageable and standardised lengths, with connections that are easy to install.

A diagrid of timbers was chosen to establish an inherently strong shell action. While the plywood sheathing at the top of the diagrid is both the ceiling and a stress layer to resist buckling, it also provides a uniform substrate for zinc roofing. The ability of plywood to serve several functions like these helped to reduce the cost of the overall roof build-up.

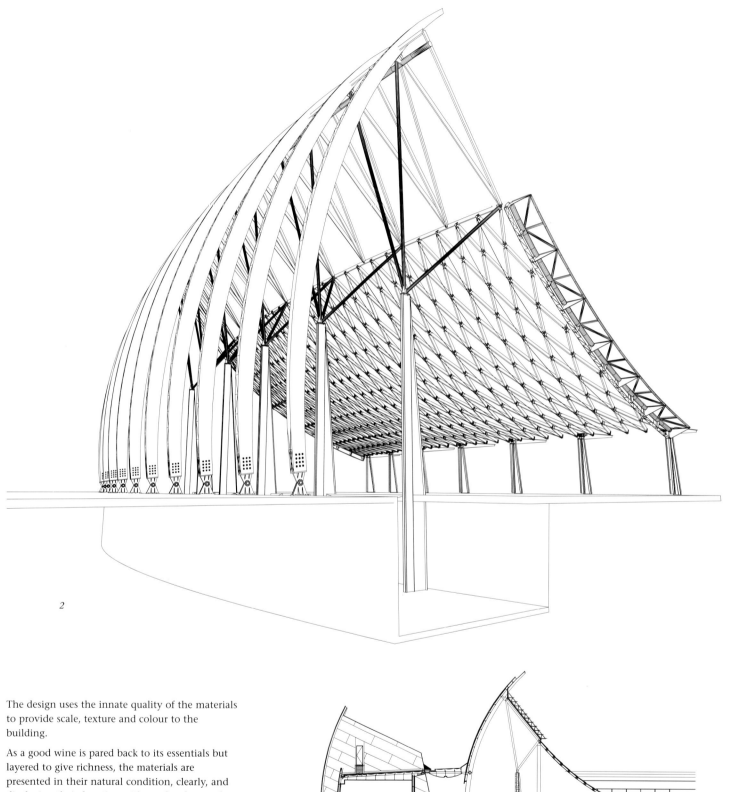

2

The design uses the innate quality of the materials to provide scale, texture and colour to the building.

As a good wine is pared back to its essentials but layered to give richness, the materials are presented in their natural condition, clearly, and displaying their function without the clutter of applied decoration.

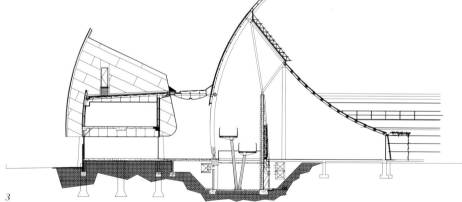

3

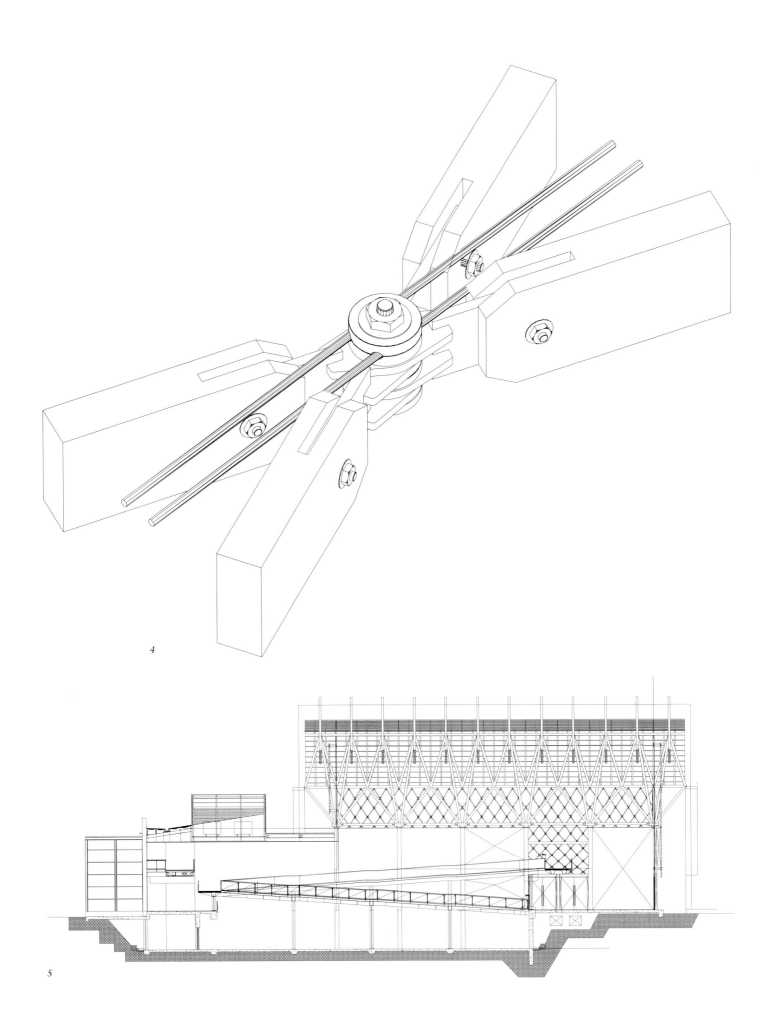

4

5

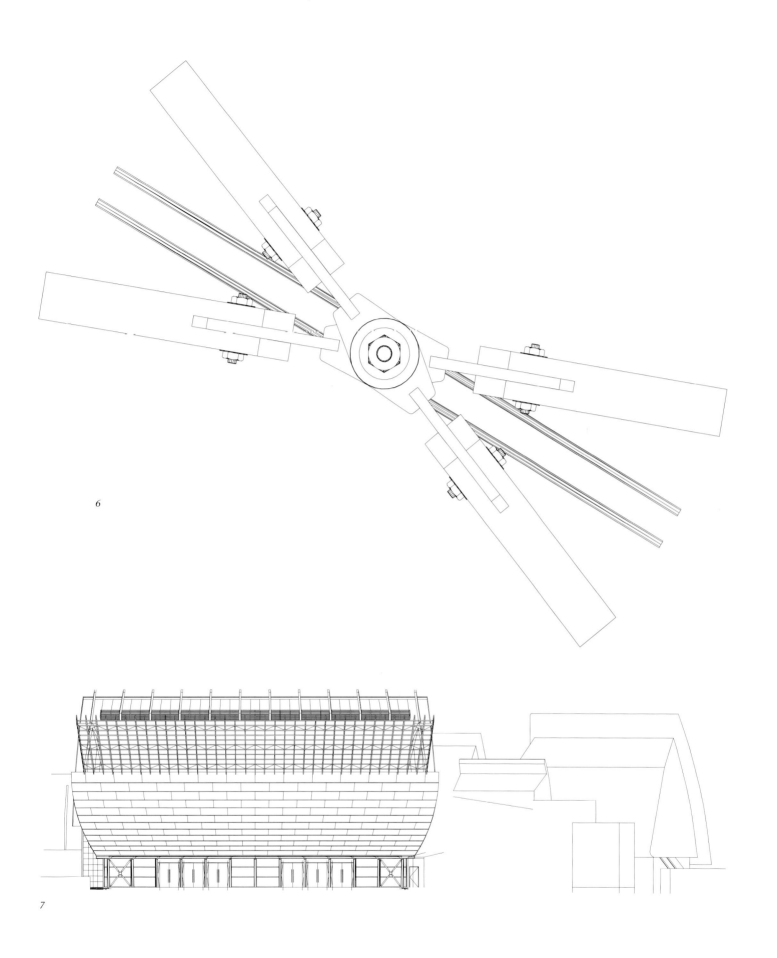

6

7

4&6 Knuckle joint detail
5 Cross section
7 Northwest elevation
Photography: Trevor Fox

BIFOLDING VERTICAL SLIDING DOORS
ALUMBRERA RESIDENCE, MUSTIQUE, ST VINCENT AND THE GRENADINES, WEST INDIES
Diamond and Schmitt Architects Incorporated

1

This residence is located on Mustique, a privately owned island in the West Indies. The 730-hectare island has been developed as one of the world's most exclusive resorts, and when fully developed, will have no more than 100 villas and a small hotel.

The residence is a five-bedroom complex covering 800 square metres. It is organised as a series of smaller pavilions and recreational facilities, which are linked by landscaped gardens and terraces, and arranged to take advantage of the views and prevailing winds on the large hilltop site. Separate components include the living pavilion with large areas for dining and entertaining; bedroom pavilion; guest suite pavilion; and kitchen pavilion, all arranged around a central terrace.

The residence takes full advantage of its beautiful site, allowing for an open-air lifestyle while providing luxurious seclusion and privacy.

Central to this open-air concept are the bifold vertical doors that are located on the central living pavilion. The tropical location requires a constant breeze to provide cooling, and the slotted doors can accommodate this need in both the open and closed positions.

1   Living room pavilion – louvred doors
2   Detail section
3   Louvred doors in closed position

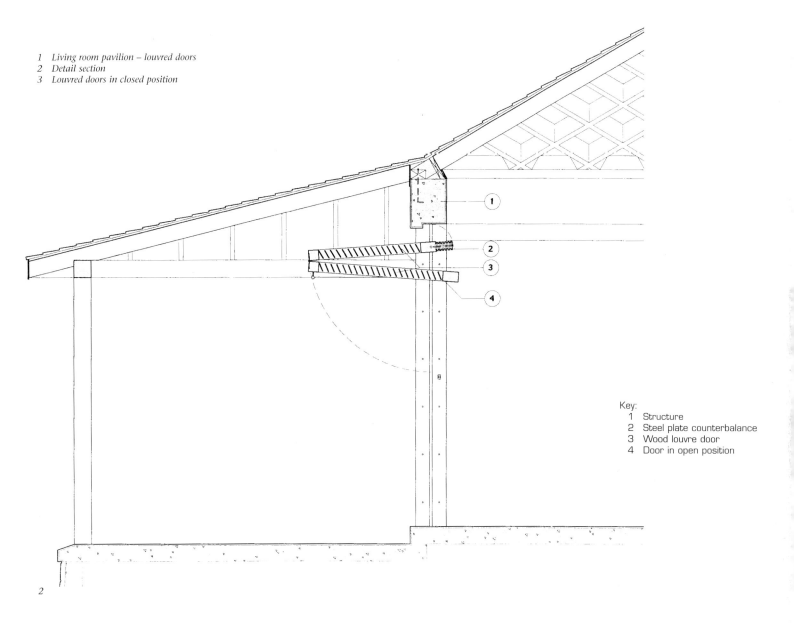

Key:
1   Structure
2   Steel plate counterbalance
3   Wood louvre door
4   Door in open position

2

The flexibility of the door system allows them to function as both door and wall. The action of the doors prevents them from disrupting furniture, and in the raised position they effectively lower the ceiling along the covered porch areas, creating a more intimate environment.

The assembly is a low-tech solution for easy maintenance in the islands where skilled labour is scarce.

3

4 Louvred doors in open and closed position
5 Living room interior
6 Living room with surrounding verandah
7 Millwork detail
Photography: Steven Evans

4

5

6

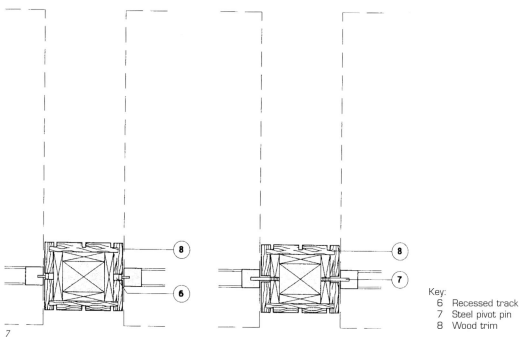

7

Key:
6 Recessed track
7 Steel pivot pin
8 Wood trim

BANQUETTE AND DECORATIVE SCREEN

THE ROSEWOOD HOTEL AND ROSEWOOD RESTAURANTS @ AL FAISALIAH COMPLEX, RIYADH, SAUDI ARABIA

Architectural Interior Designer: DiLeonardo International, Inc.

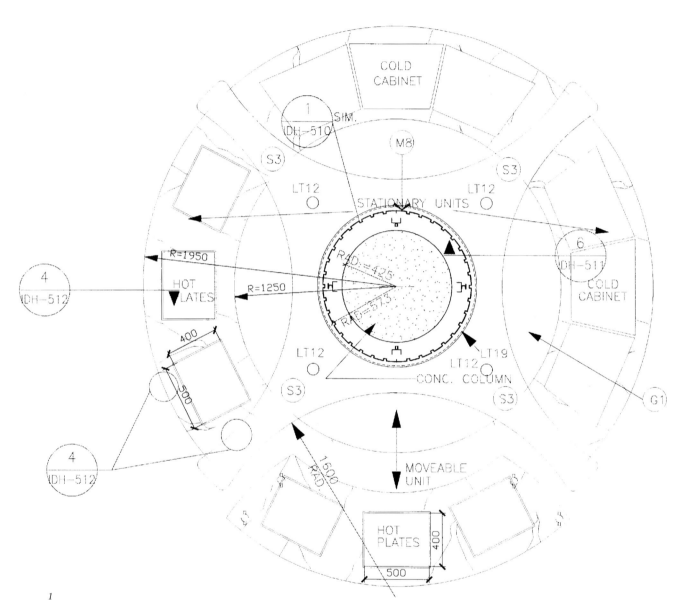

1

The Al Faisaliah Hotel, part of Dallas-based Rosewood Hotels and Resorts, offers a tradition of fine dining in various eating areas.

The challenge met by the design team was to combine the classic elegance associated with the Rosewood name with the very contemporary image of this development. Richness, clarity and attention to detail are evident at every level of the project.

The 'Cristal Restaurant' has been hailed as one of the finest restaurants in Riyadh. It features structural columns clad in Brazilian mahogany that slant slightly towards each end. This shape is mirrored by large, mounted, cast-glass decorative screens which divide the seating groups.

The banquettes have been designed to create a sense of privacy within the large open plan. Each banquette is constructed around a fluted bronze column and allows for four intimate groupings.

2

1　Plan buffet bar
2　Banquettes designed to create sense of privacy within large open plan. Each is constructed around fluted bronze column and allows for four intimate groupings
3　Elevation buffet bar
4　Section buffet bar

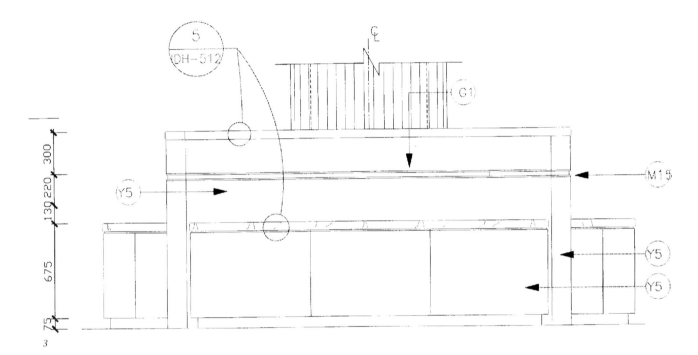

3

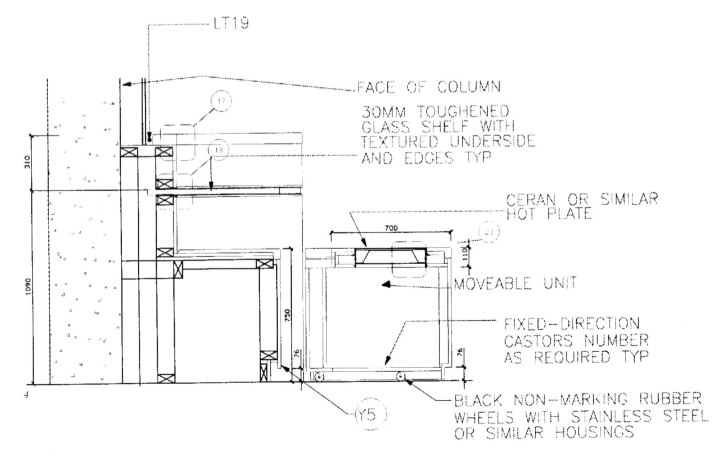

LT19

FACE OF COLUMN

30MM TOUGHENED GLASS SHELF WITH TEXTURED UNDERSIDE AND EDGES TYP

CERAN OR SIMILAR HOT PLATE

MOVEABLE UNIT

FIXED-DIRECTION CASTORS NUMBER AS REQUIRED TYP

BLACK NON-MARKING RUBBER WHEELS WITH STAINLESS STEEL OR SIMILAR HOUSINGS

4

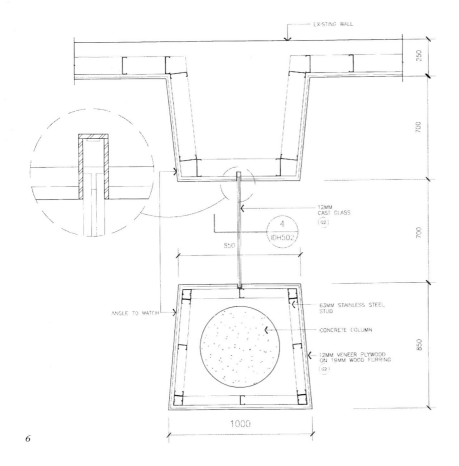

EXISTING WALL

250

700

700

12MM
CAST GLASS
(G2)

$\dfrac{4}{IDH502}$

850

550

ANGLE TO MATCH

63MM STAINLESS STEEL
STUD

CONCRETE COLUMN

12MM VENEER PLYWOOD
ON 19MM WOOD FURRING
(G2)

1000

6

Opposite:
*Structural columns clad in Brazilian
mahogany slant slightly towards each
end. This shape is mirrored by large
cast-glass mounted between to create
visual screens between seating groups*
6 *Plan section at decorative screen and
column*
7 *Elevation*
Photography: Mike Wilson

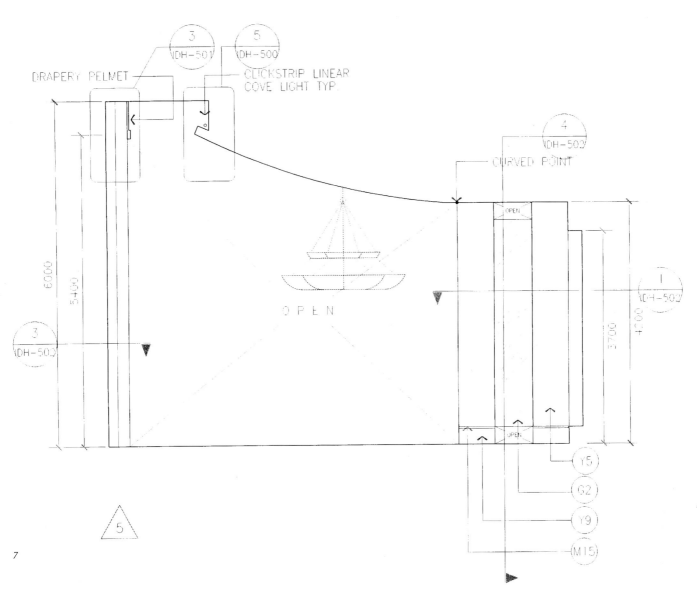

$\dfrac{3}{IDH-501}$ $\dfrac{5}{IDH-500}$

DRAPERY PELMET

CLICKSTRIP LINEAR
COVE LIGHT TYP.

$\dfrac{4}{IDH-502}$

CURVED POINT

$\dfrac{3}{IDH-502}$

6000

5400

OPEN

OPEN

3700

4000

$\dfrac{1}{IDH-502}$

OPEN

Y5

G2

Y9

M15

5

7

GUEST CORRIDOR, MONUMENTAL STAIR
AND REGISTRATION DESK

THE ROSEWOOD HOTEL AND ROSEWOOD RESTAURANTS @ AL FAISALIAH COMPLEX, RIYADH, SAUDI ARABIA
Architectural Interior Designer: DiLeonardo International, Inc.

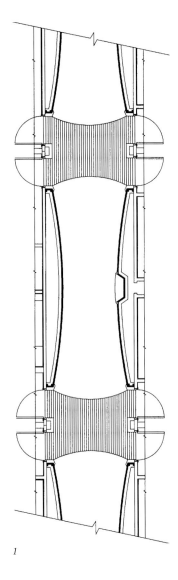

1

2

1 Typical corridor plan
2 Elliptical forms of guest corridor
   shortens perceived length of corridor
   and allows for decorative niches and
   monolithic casework at guest entry.
   Rear-lit cove signals entry
3 Typical corridor elevation
4–6 Corridor wall detail
7 Corridor chair rail detail

The Al Faisaliah Complex has at its core a sense of synergy created through diverse and multiple talents. The result is a seamless flow from one space to another, combined with a sense of subtly re-occurring elements which have shaped the project.

The sophistication of this hospitality complex is evident in the juxtaposition of rich materials. Refined deep woods are combined with warm but slightly irregular limestone. The shell wraps the space, creating a liner for the building as a hole. The elliptical geometries found in the forms of the buildings themselves are repeated throughout many spaces.

Continuity is evident in the guestroom corridors as well as the guestrooms.

Corridors undulate in elliptical patterns to add interest and shorten their perceived length.

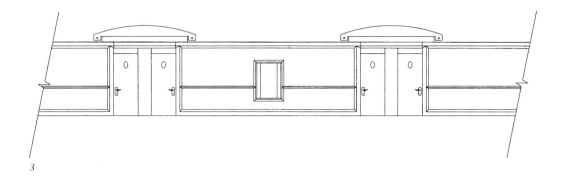

3

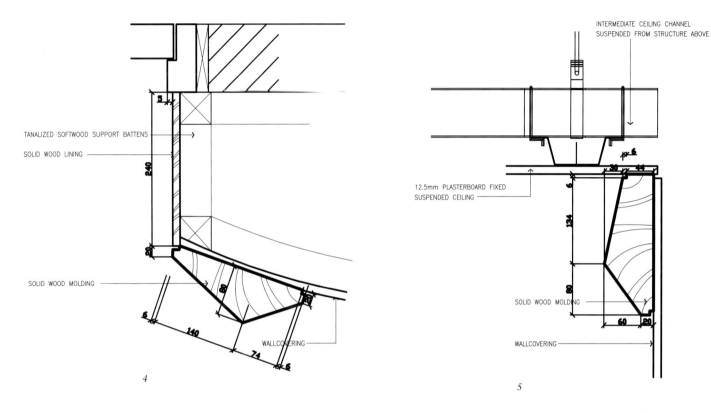

TANALIZED SOFTWOOD SUPPORT BATTENS

SOLID WOOD LINING

SOLID WOOD MOLDING

WALLCOVERING

4

INTERMEDIATE CEILING CHANNEL
SUSPENDED FROM STRUCTURE ABOVE

12.5mm PLASTERBOARD FIXED
SUSPENDED CEILING

SOLID WOOD MOLDING

WALLCOVERING

5

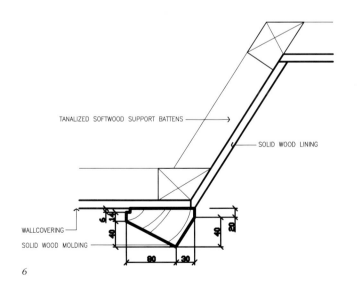

TANALIZED SOFTWOOD SUPPORT BATTENS

SOLID WOOD LINING

WALLCOVERING

SOLID WOOD MOLDING

6

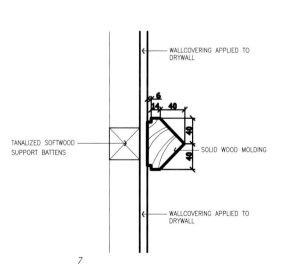

WALLCOVERING APPLIED TO
DRYWALL

TANALIZED SOFTWOOD
SUPPORT BATTENS

SOLID WOOD MOLDING

WALLCOVERING APPLIED TO
DRYWALL

7

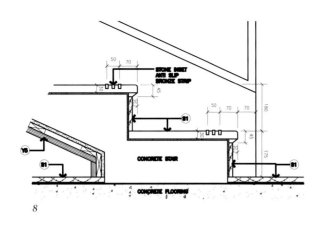

8

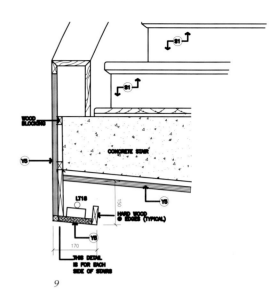

9

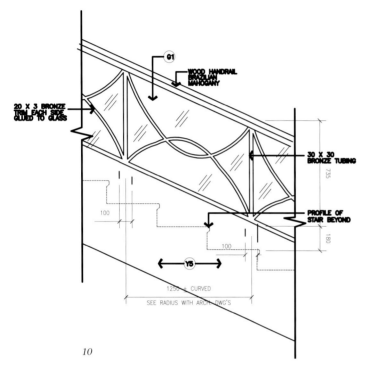

10

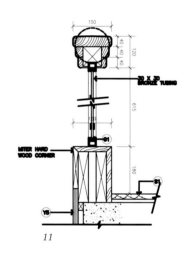

11

8 Riser section at atrium
9 Section at atrium
10 Stair elevation
11 Handrail detail at atrium
12 Plan
13 Elevation at connector line
14 Stair

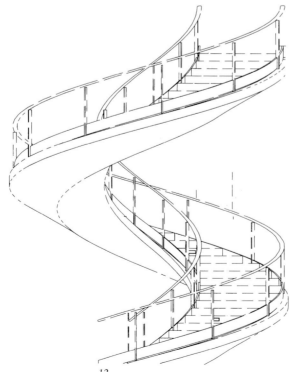

12

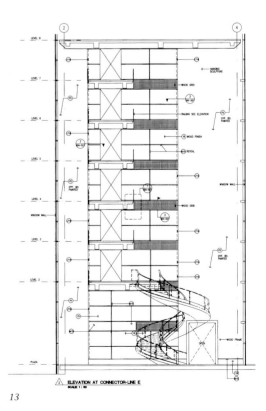

ELEVATION AT CONNECTOR-LINE E
SCALE 1 : 50

13

14

Brazilian mahogany, a timber commonly used throughout the hotel, is combined with bronze tubing to create the banisters for the atrium stairs.

The monumental staircase is housed within an eight-storey atrium and is clad in Portuguese limestone. Each step features bronze strips to ensure traction. The continuous underside of the stair is clad in mahogany and is lit from each side, and the rail is fabricated in tempered glass and bronze.

Black granite, frosted glass, bronze and plywood has been used to achieve a stately result in the registration desk.

15 Registration desk consists of Brazilian mahogany, bronze and up-lit frosted glass. Fins resemble shape of tower architecture while outlining registration stations

16 Registration desk plan

17 Registration desk rear elevation

18&19 Sections

Photography: Mike Wilson

15

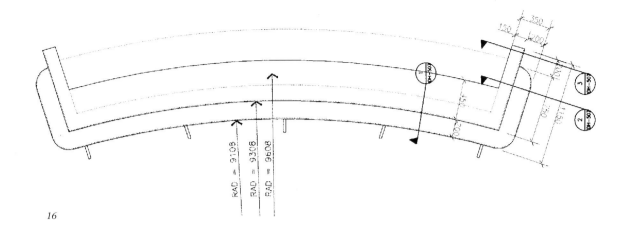

16

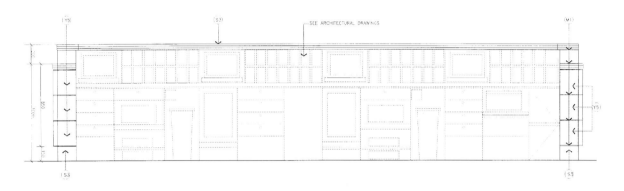

17

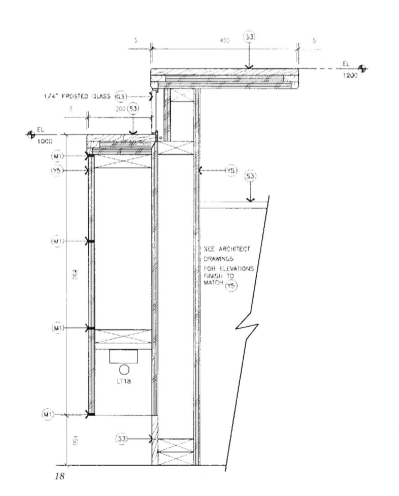

18

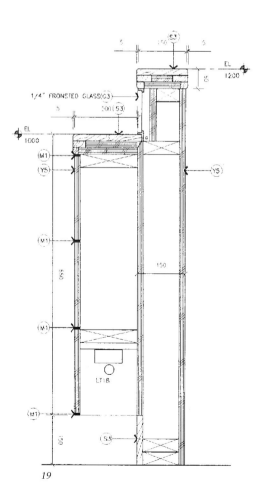

19

SPA WATERWALL
THE ROSEWOOD HOTEL AND ROSEWOOD RESTAURANTS @ AL FAISALIAH COMPLEX, RIYADH, SAUDI ARABIA
Architectural Interior Designer: DiLeonardo International, Inc.

1

The hospitality complex is a sophisticated, contemporary experience. The design was approached so as to create a sense of continuity and harmony with the space, as well as with the architecture.

The designers met the challenge of combining the classic elegance associated with the Rosewood name with the very contemporary image of this development. A richness enters each aspect of the project, and this is visible in the attention to detail across the design.

The spa waterwall is more than symbolic of the holistic experience of the Al Faisaliah complex. It is an elegant and essential aspect of the approach to hospitality experienced by guests and residents.

An audio-visual effect is created by the spa waterwall. The cast-glass tiles are mounted on various planes, are back-lit, and can be felt above and below the surface of the water. The overall result is sensuous and timeless.

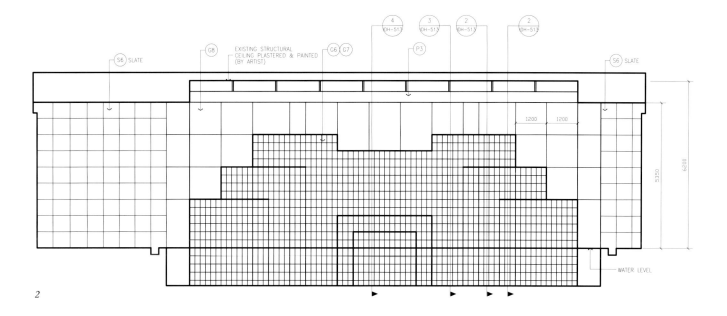

2

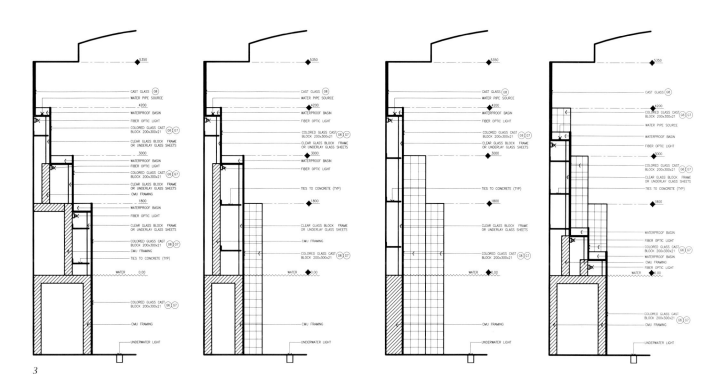

3

1 Cast-glass tiles mounted on differing
   planes, rear-lit with water cascading from
   each edge to create audio-visual effect.
   Tiles can be felt both above and below the
   surface of the water
2 Elevation at spa fountain wall
3 Section
Photography: Mike Wilson

GLASS DOME
JEFFERSON COUNTY COURTS AND ADMINISTRATION BUILDING, GOLDEN, COLORADO, USA
Fentress Bradburn Architects

1

2

The design of the Jefferson County Courts and Administration Building sought to create an icon that would return the county seat to its former prominence as the heart of the community. The plan splits the facility's two major functions into separate arcs that are connected by a 38-metre-high glass rotunda.

County officials wanted a building with a timeless character, achieved in part by topping the building's central atrium with a glass dome. The dome, in addition to the atrium's east and west glass façade, is a metaphor for open and accessible government.

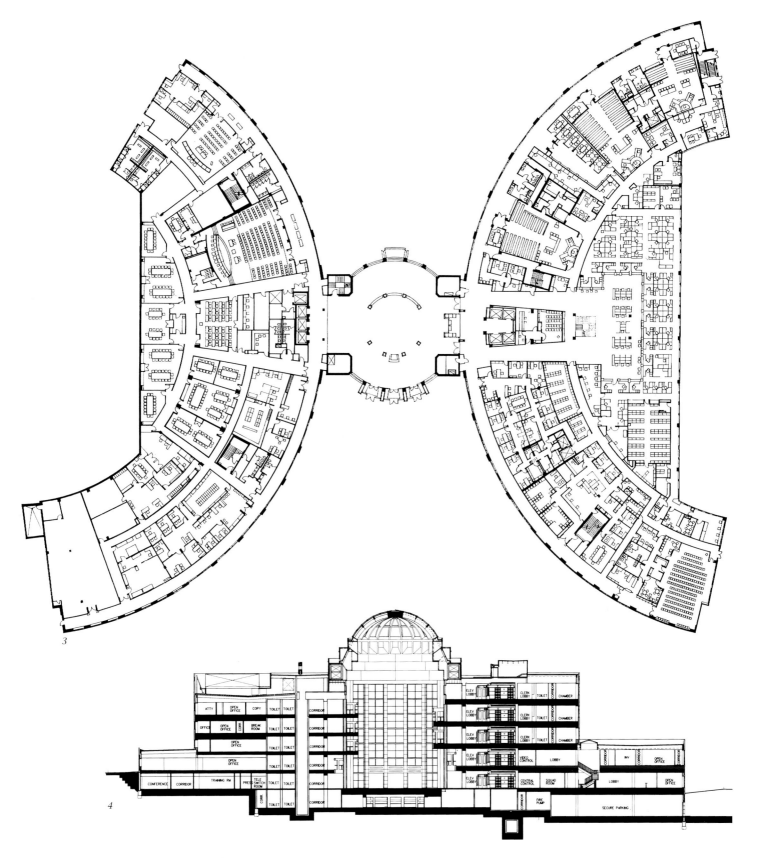

3

4

Construction of the dome required the novel application of a box truss that is curved in plan, created by structural engineers Richard Weingardt Consultants, Inc. This circular truss is the first time a tube structure had been used as a horizontal tension ring to support both the vertical and thrust forces of the dome. The ring is supported on only four piers and floats freely, moving independently of the adjacent wings.

1 Building with night lighting
2 Rotunda at sunrise, showing transparency of façade and dome
3 Rotunda connects two arced wings. County administration and chambers on left; and county courts on the right
4 Building section

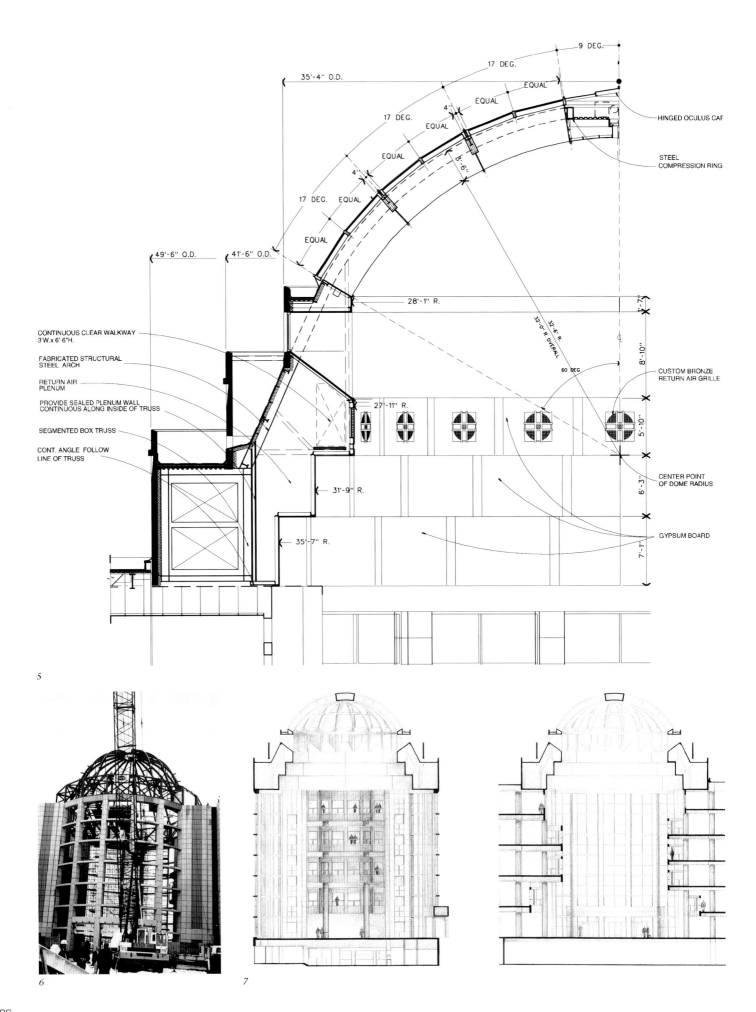

9 DEG.

35'-4" O.D.

17 DEG.

EQUAL

HINGED OCULUS CAP

17 DEG.

4'

EQUAL

STEEL
COMPRESSION RING

EQUAL

6'-6"

49'-6" O.D.

41'-6" O.D.

EQUAL

4'

EQUAL

17 DEG.

EQUAL

EQUAL

28'-1" R.

1'-7"

CONTINUOUS CLEAR WALKWAY
3'W. x 6'-6"H.

32'-6" R.

32'-0" R OVERALL

8'-10"

FABRICATED STRUCTURAL
STEEL ARCH

60 DEG

CUSTOM BRONZE
RETURN AIR GRILLE

RETURN AIR
PLENUM

27'-11" R.

PROVIDE SEALED PLENUM WALL
CONTINUOUS ALONG INSIDE OF TRUSS

5'-10"

SEGMENTED BOX TRUSS

CONT. ANGLE FOLLOW
LINE OF TRUSS

CENTER POINT
OF DOME RADIUS

6'-3"

31'-9" R.

GYPSUM BOARD

35'-7" R.

7'-1"

5

6

7

8

The circular shape of the truss not only gives it added stiffness and strength, but also distributes the weight of the dome evenly around the ring, thus preventing the truss tube from bowing inward. Where a rectilinear truss would have required horizontal internal diagonal bracing, the tension-ring tube could be kept hollow in order to carry ductwork. Return air from the top of the rotunda is circulated to the ductwork by way of custom bronze grilles just below the dome.

The ribs of the dome were kept inside in order to create a glass 'cap' on the exterior. A custom window-washing platform services the glass underside of the dome.

5 *Section of glass dome*
6 *Construction photo showing tension-ring truss atop rotunda*
7 *Two elevations of rotunda*
8 *Design concept, interior of the atrium and dome*

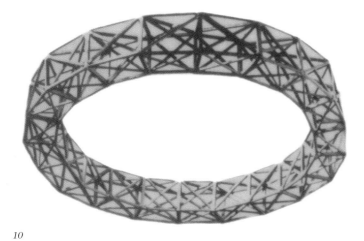

10

11

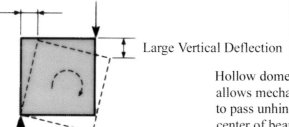

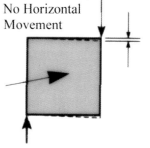

PROBLEM

Two-dimensional tube structure allows rotation

Horizontal Movement

Weight of Dome & Snow Loads (at inside face of tube)

Large Vertical Deflection

Hollow dome support beam allows mechanical ductwork to pass unhindered through center of beam. Elimination of rotation prevents damage to mechanical ductwork.

Support (at outside face of tube)

Dome Loads

Rotation

Supports (at only four locations)

SOLUTION

Three-dimensional circular tube

ring prevents rotation.

Weight of Dome & Snow Loads (at inside face of tube)

No Horizontal Movement

Less than 1/8 inch Vertical Deflection

Support (at outside face of tube)

Dome Loads

No Rotation with Circular Tube

Supports (at only four locations)

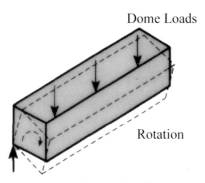

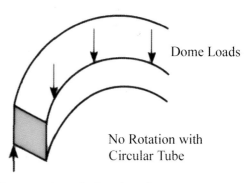

12

SPHERES
JEFFERSON COUNTY COURTS AND ADMINISTRATION BUILDING, GOLDEN, COLORADO, USA
Fentress Bradburn Architects

1

1   *Rotunda connecting two arching wings; decorative spheres to each side of rotunda*
2   *Construction drawings of spheres*
3   *Close-up of pier topped by sphere*

The design of the Jefferson County Courts and Administration Building created an icon that returned the county seat to its former prominence as the heart of the community. The plan splits the facility's major functions into two arcs that are connected by a 38-metre-high glass rotunda.

County officials sought a timeless design that would work in harmony with the circular shapes of other buildings on the county government campus.

Among the design elements that create this ceremonial quality are the decorative spheres that grace the top of the four piers on which the glass

dome of the rotunda rests. Like the dome of the building's rotunda, the embraced sphere is a form that has been used historically to evoke universal qualities and to represent civic purpose.

Each sphere rests in a curved steel saddle atop one of the rotunda's four precast piers. Each is encircled by a curved plate in the form of a built-up circular I-beam that surrounds the sphere at mid-height, and gives the appearance of a double ring. This is supported by four steel plates, three of which rest on the pier and one of which attaches to a plate that is embedded in the face of the pier and projects out at an angle.

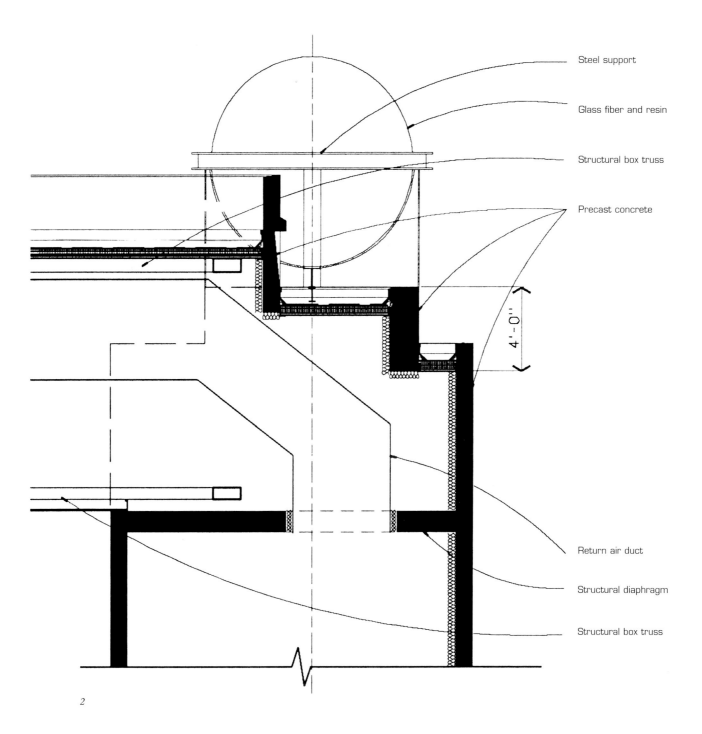

Steel support

Glass fiber and resin

Structural box truss

Precast concrete

4'-0"

Return air duct

Structural diaphragm

Structural box truss

2

Despite cost-cutting measures, the architects were able to retain the spheres in the overall design by an inventive use of materials. Each sphere is a hollow fibreglass and resin shell on which automotive paint was used to approximate a bronze appearance.

3

Opposite:
Rotunda, decorative spheres atop piers to either side
5   Construction drawings of spheres
Photography: Nick Merrick, Hedrich-Blessing

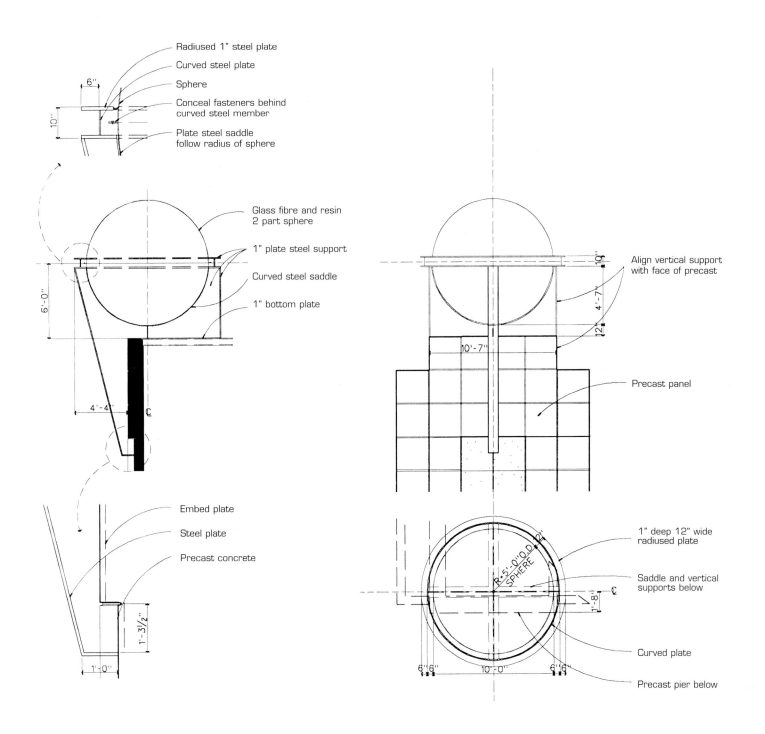

Radiused 1" steel plate

Curved steel plate

Sphere

Conceal fasteners behind
curved steel member

Plate steel saddle
follow radius of sphere

6"

10"

Glass fibre and resin
2 part sphere

1" plate steel support

Curved steel saddle

1" bottom plate

6'-0"

4'-4"

Embed plate

Steel plate

Precast concrete

1'-3 1/2"

1'-0"

Align vertical support
with face of precast

10'-7"

19"

4'-7"

12"

Precast panel

1" deep 12" wide
radiused plate

Saddle and vertical
supports below

Curved plate

Precast pier below

R·5'-0" O.D.
SPHERE

2"

1'-8"

6"6"

10'-0"

6"6"

GLAZED ATRIUM ROOF
BRITISH LIBRARY OF POLITICAL AND ECONOMIC SCIENCE, LONDON SCHOOL OF ECONOMICS, LONDON, UK
Foster and Partners

1

The London School of Economics and Political Science has the world's largest and most important social sciences library. The redevelopment of the library building safeguards the future of the school's four million books by improving environmental standards, and provides 500 extra student workplaces and new accommodation for the school's research centre.

Built in 1914, the Lionel Robbins building was converted into a library in 1973. The renovation retains the basic building fabric and maintains the integrity of the façades, although the windows have been replaced.

A central atrium has been created by removing the façades of an internal lightwell and extending the floor-plates to encircle a cylindrical space. This increases the floor area, improves circulation and introduces daylight into the heart of the building. The atrium has been driven through to the basement and houses a helical ramp and a pair of glass lifts, which provide the main vertical circulation through the building.

A dome caps the atrium. It has a glazed section cut at an angle to admit north light, allowing maximum daylight penetration without problems of glare and solar gain. The dome also assists

1 Interior view of cylindrical atrium showing
   glass lifts leading up to glazed dome cap
2 Interior view of book stacks and study
   areas radiating from the central atrium
3 Cross section
4 Concept sketch

2

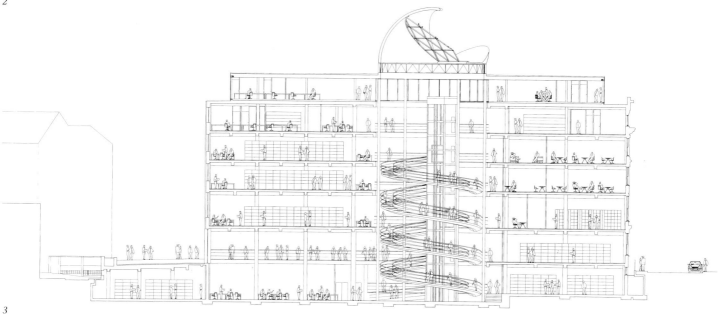

3

natural ventilation: air drawn in through windows at the perimeter of the library rises as it worms and escapes through vents in the dome's glazing.

Bookshelves radiate from the atrium to create clearly defined passageways, and quiet study areas are positioned at the perimeter of each floor. A new fifth floor accommodates the Research Centre, which has its own entrance.

4

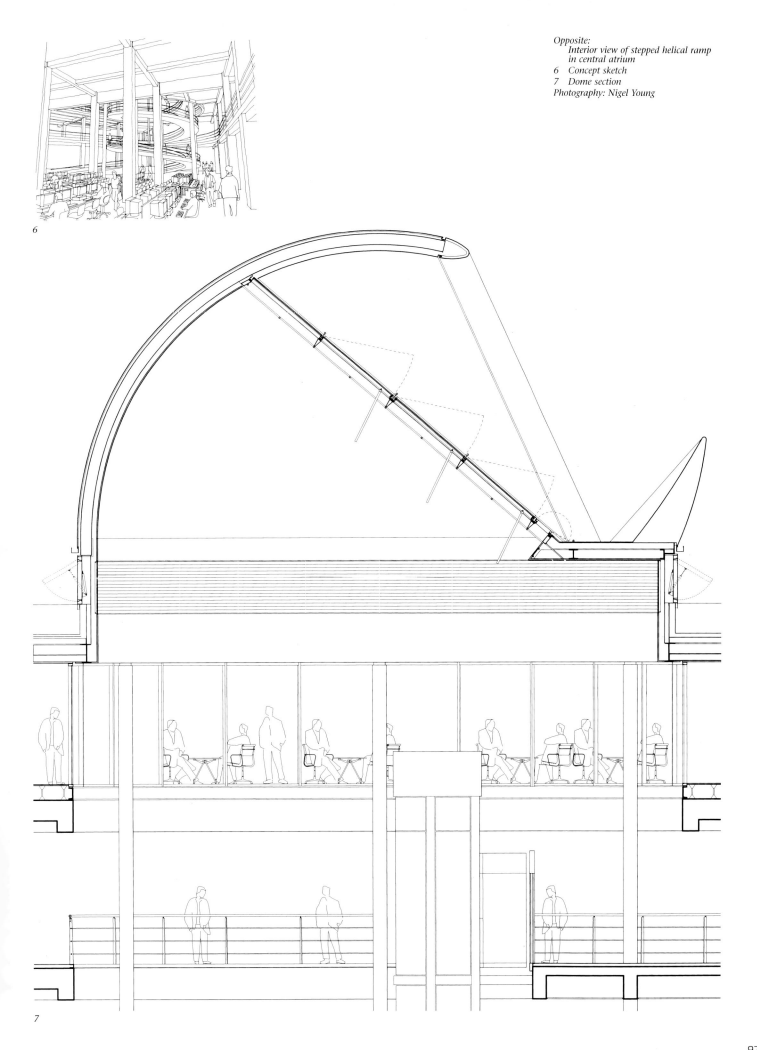

Opposite:
*Interior view of stepped helical ramp
in central atrium*
6   *Concept sketch*
7   *Dome section*
Photography: Nigel Young

6

7

GLAZED CANOPY
QUEEN ELIZABETH II GREAT COURT AT THE BRITISH MUSEUM, LONDON, UK
Foster and Partners

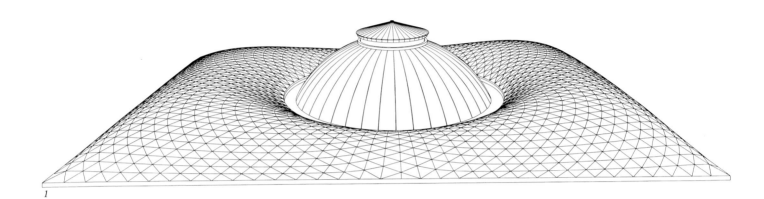

1

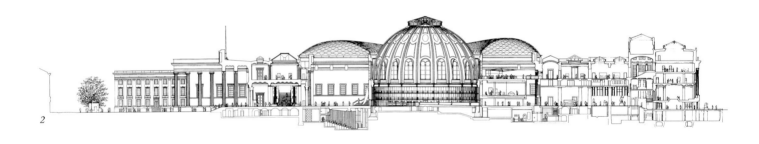

2

3

The courtyard at the centre of the British Museum was one of London's long-lost spaces. Originally an open garden, soon after its completion in the 19th century it was filled by the round Reading Room and its associated bookstacks. Without this space the museum was like a city without a park. This project is about its re-invention.

The British Museum receives up to six million visitors annually, making it more popular than the Louvre in Paris or the Metropolitan Museum of Art in New York. In the absence of a centralised circulation system this degree of popularity caused a critical level of congestion throughout the building and created a frustrating experience for the visitor.

The departure of the British Library to St Pancras in March 1998 provided the opportunity to recapture the courtyard and greatly enhance the museum's facilities for coming generations. The clutter of bookstacks that filled the courtyard has been cleared away to create a new public heart to the building, while the Reading Room has been restored and put to new use as an information centre and library of world cultures. For the first time in its history this magnificent space – its dome larger than that of St Paul's – is open to all.

The Great Court is entered from the museum's principal level, and connects all the surrounding galleries. Within the space there are information

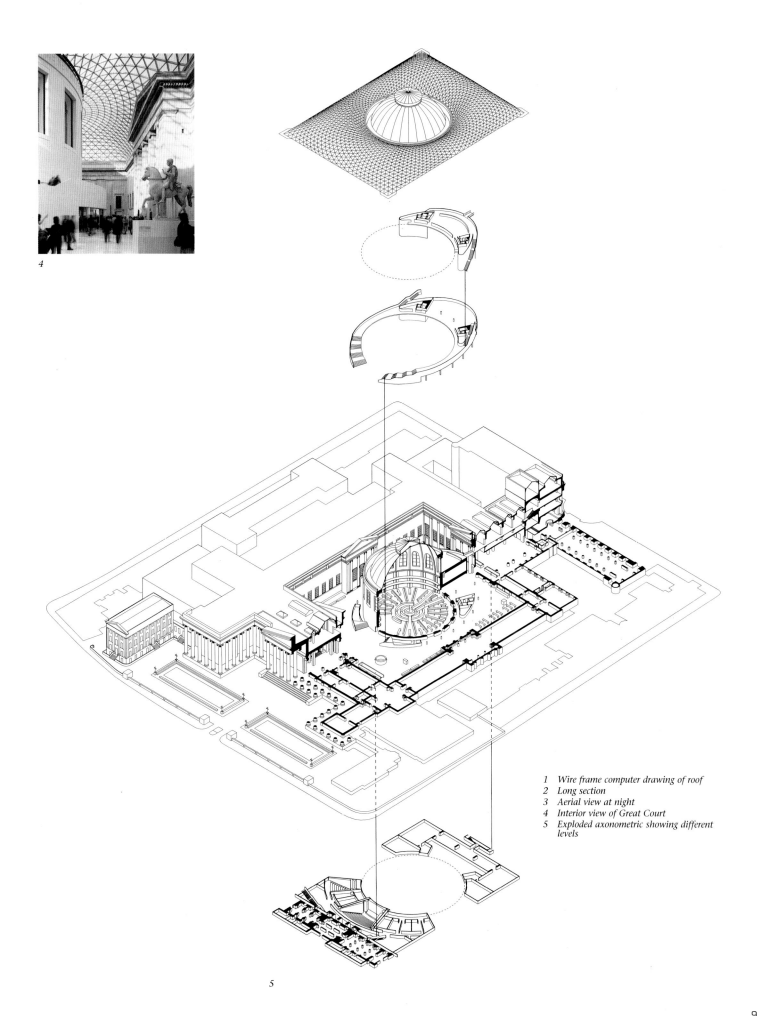

1 Wire frame computer drawing of roof
2 Long section
3 Aerial view at night
4 Interior view of Great Court
5 Exploded axonometric showing different
   levels

4

5

Opposite:
Interior detail of window looking into Reading Room towards the cupola
7 Reading and Great Court, ground floor level
8 General interior view of Great Court and Reading Room

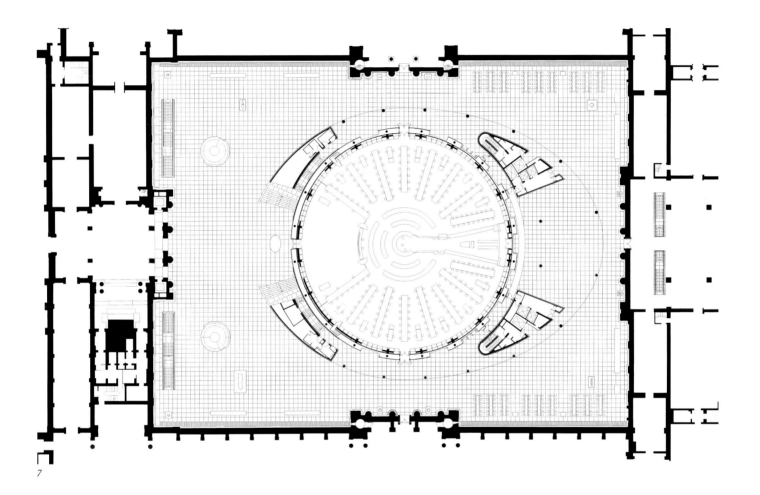

7

points, a book shop and a café. Two broad staircases encircling the Reading Room lead to two mezzanine levels, ovoid in plan, which provide a gallery for temporary exhibitions with a restaurant above. Below the level of the court are the Sainsbury African Galleries, an education centre with two auditoria, and new facilities for school children.

The glazed canopy that makes all this possible is a fusion of state-of-the-art engineering and economy of form. Its unique triangulated geometry is designed to span the irregular gap between the drum of the Reading Room and the restored courtyard façades. The lattice steel shell forms both the primary structure and the framing

for the glazing system, which is designed to maximise daylight and reduce solar gain.

The Great Court is the largest enclosed public space in Europe. As a cultural square, it lies on a new pedestrian route from the British Library in the north to Covent Garden and the river in the south. To complement the Great Court, the museum's forecourt has been freed from cars and restored to form a new public space. Both are open to the public from early in the morning to late at night, creating a major amenity for London.

8

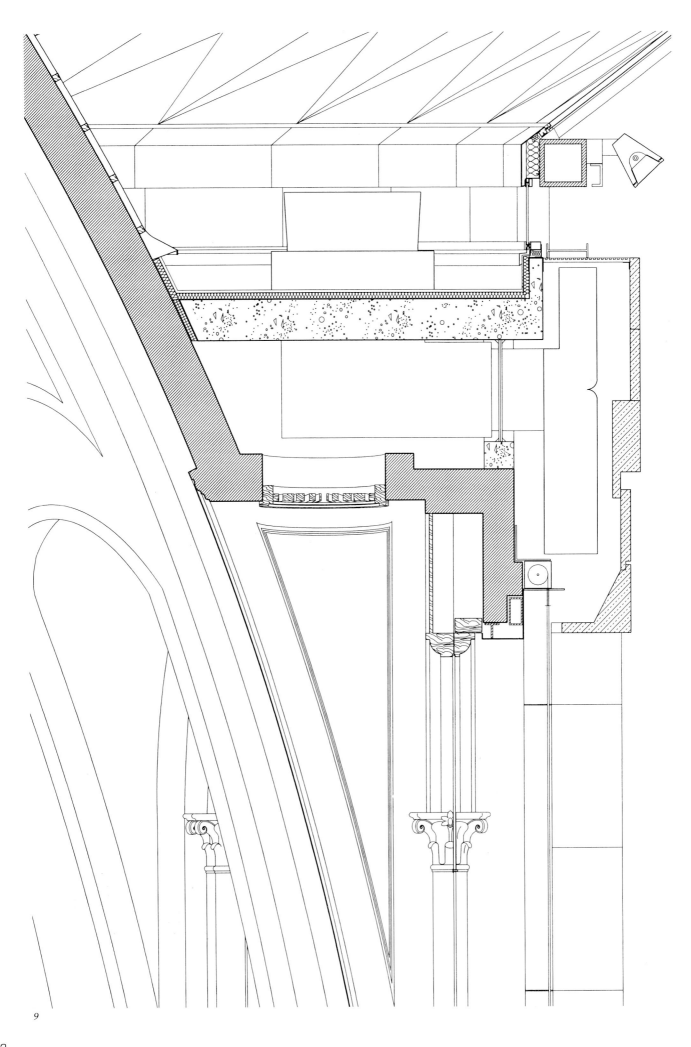

10

11

12

13

14 *Detail of perimeter of Great Court*
Opposite:
    Interior detail of Great Court at night
Photography: Nigel Young, Foster and Partners

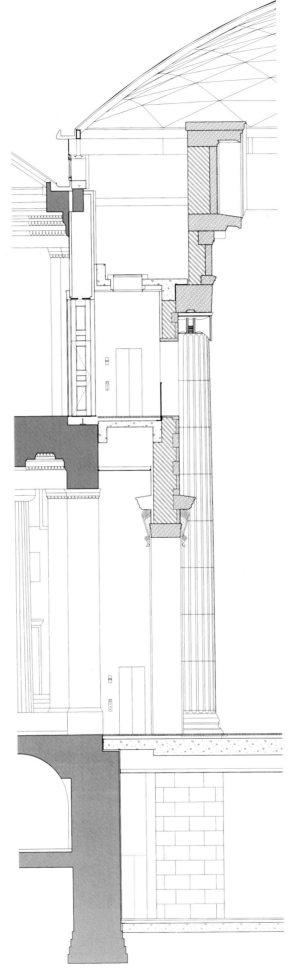

14

GLASS PANELS WITH STAINLESS STEEL SPIDER CONNECTIONS

AMERICAN BIBLE SOCIETY, NEW YORK, NEW YORK, USA

Fox & Fowle Architects

1

2

When constructed, the American Bible Society's pre-existing headquarters building, a 1960s modern classic, was sited back from the Broadway street line to form a plaza. The original neighbouring low-rise buildings have since been demolished and replaced by high-rises, resulting in a lack of presence and identity.

The Fox & Fowle solution brought a fresh new presence to the Broadway façade; conveyed the society's message to the public; made the building, bookstore and gallery inviting to the public; revitalised the interior working spaces; and upgraded systems to save energy and improve the environment.

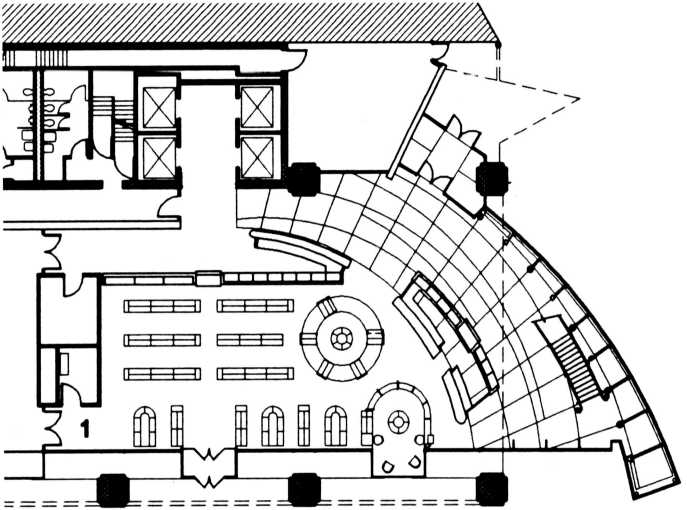

3

Carefully sculpted so as not to diminish the integrity of the original structure, an all-glass pavilion form starts with a dramatic sweep through the first floor, and evolves into a flared volume that extends onto the plaza. The structurally glazed pavilion is composed of carefully proportioned and shaped pieces of monolithic glass, secured by stainless steel 'spider' connections, the first used in New York City.

From the exterior, the society's message is conveyed through a multi-screen video system, etched inscriptions on the glass of 'In the Beginning' in the 67 languages published by the society, and projected images, all of which are integrated with the high-tech glass and steel structure to create a media wall.

The carefully lit pavilion glows at night, animated by a bank of video monitors incorporated into the curve of the façade. The transparency and lightness of the pavilion let the eye of the passerby easily penetrate the interior space and complements, rather than competes with, the forceful façade of the building beyond.

1 View of pavilion showing media wall and stairs to second floor gallery
2 Bird's eye view of pavilion addition
3 Ground floor plan
4 View of media wall and spider connections from interior

5

TWO-PART ROOFING STRUCTURE
SEIBU DOME, TOKOROZAWA, JAPAN
Kajima Design

1

1   Interior upon completion
2&3 Cross section
4   Roof plan
Following pages:
     Raising the membrane roof

The 40,000-square-metre roof of the Saibu Dome was designed to span a pre-existing baseball stadium and make it semi-outdoor.

The large roof is comprised of two distinct parts. A ring-shaped metallic roof structure, with high insulation and acoustical qualities, covers the seating area. The pitch area is covered by a single-layer Teflon membrane that draws in daylight to illuminate the field.

Ventilation is a design feature of the two-part roof. A mechanism located where the two parts of the dome meet releases hot air collected in the upper section. The lower section of the large roof, which tilts 5 degrees, is completely open to aid ventilation of the large space.

Construction of the roof took place over two off-seasons. The first phase saw the completion of the metallic ring over the seating. The Teflon membrane was installed in the period of the following off-season.

The two-part roof concept allowed the construction of the roof to take place without interrupting the regular baseball season, and proved the best solution for the various demands of the design.

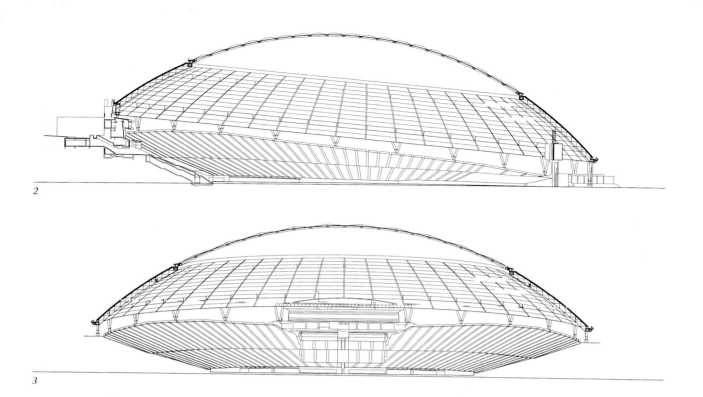

2

3

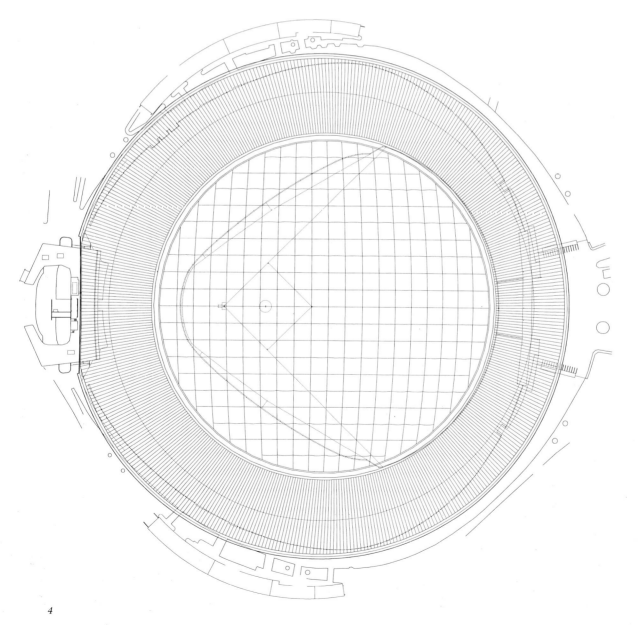

4

Opposite:
Aerial view of dome from east, showing Mt Fuji
7 *Roofing structure*
8 *Seibu Dome located in wooded and mountainous setting*
9 *Open sides of dome*
Photography: Sadamu Saito

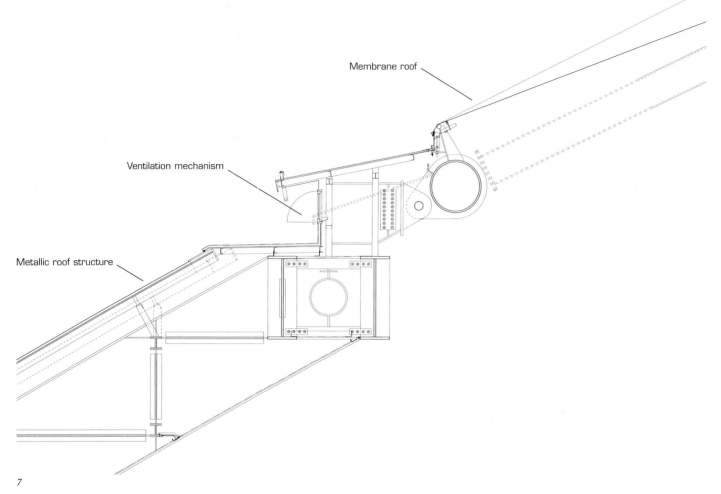

Membrane roof

Ventilation mechanism

Metallic roof structure

7

8

9

VERTICAL MULLIONS AND GLASS FINS
GANNETT/USA TODAY CORPORATE HEADQUARTERS, McLEAN, VIRGINIA, USA
Kohn Pedersen Fox Associates PC

1

2

The project consists of a new headquarters of 74,322 square metres for 'Gannett' and 'USA Today' on a 12-hectare site outside Washington, DC. This represents a corporate move from an urban high-rise work environment to a suburban location, providing considerable potential for site amenities, and the ability to design a more flexible space to facilitate integrating new technology for a more productive work environment.

The project consists of two linear towers on a common base, with 'USA Today' and 'Gannett' corporate structures spiralling up to enclose an exterior 'town square'. The single-loaded

circulation system, expressed on the courtyard side of the buildings above, activates this inner space, creating a sense of community for the 'Gannett' and 'USA Today' staff at the heart of the complex.

The building provides for three basic functional program elements: newsroom and production areas, typical office areas and common facilities. Common spaces are distributed along the entry level of the complex, with flexible, deep newsroom and production spaces in high-ceiling areas on podium levels two and three.

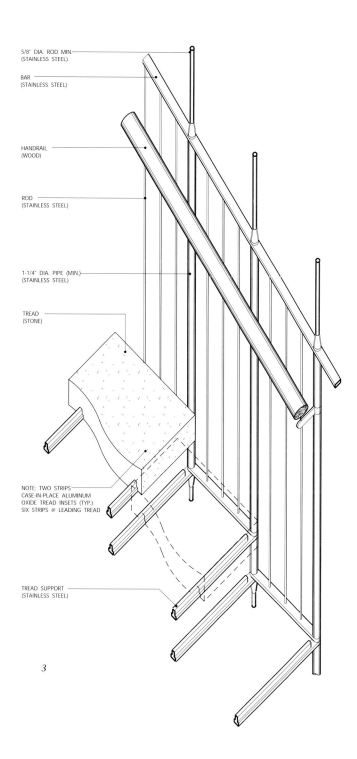

5/8" DIA. ROD MIN.
(STAINLESS STEEL)

BAR
(STAINLESS STEEL)

HANDRAIL
(WOOD)

ROD
(STAINLESS STEEL)

1-1/4" DIA. PIPE (MIN.)
(STAINLESS STEEL)

TREAD
(STONE)

NOTE: TWO STRIPS
CASE-IN-PLACE ALUMINUM
OXIDE TREAD INSETS (TYP.)
SIX STRIPS @ LEADING TREAD

TREAD SUPPORT
(STAINLESS STEEL)

3

4

5

Typical office spaces are located above in linear towers, designed with flexibility for departmental change, and oriented on the site to maximise views.

The design orients the community space and the complex as a whole towards the pond at the centre of the site, allowing the southern orientation to maximise sunlight into the exterior courtyard and adjacent terraces. Landscaping is used to reinforce the site features and as a buffer to noise along the adjacent highways.

1 'Harp' stair
2 'Gannett' building viewed from 'USA Today', with lobby and atrium in foreground
3 Axonometric of stair detail
4 View from south
5 'Harp' stair detail

6 Elevation at handrail
7 Section at pool
Opposite:
    'Harp' stair detail

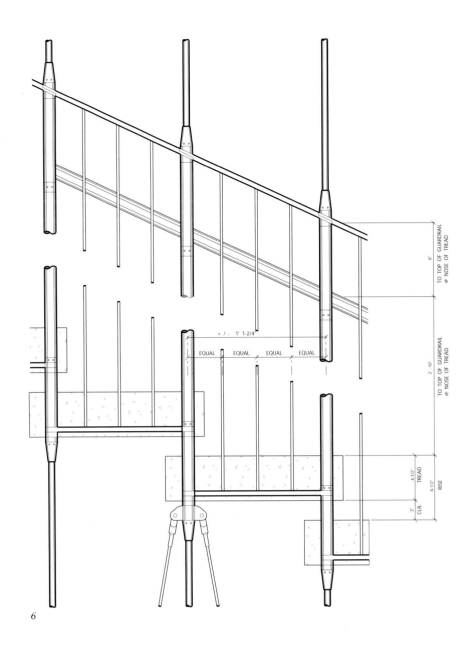

6

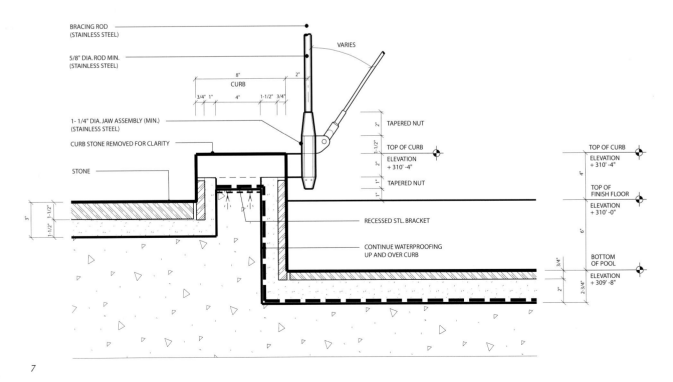

BRACING ROD
(STAINLESS STEEL)

5/8" DIA. ROD MIN.
(STAINLESS STEEL)

1- 1/4" DIA. JAW ASSEMBLY (MIN.)
(STAINLESS STEEL)

CURB STONE REMOVED FOR CLARITY

STONE

VARIES

CURB
8"   2"
3/4" 1"   4"   1-1/2" 3/4"

2"   TAPERED NUT
1-1/2"   TOP OF CURB
2"   ELEVATION
        + 310' -4"
1"   TAPERED NUT

RECESSED STL. BRACKET

CONTINUE WATERPROOFING
UP AND OVER CURB

TOP OF CURB
ELEVATION
+ 310' -4"

TOP OF
FINISH FLOOR
ELEVATION
+ 310' -0"

BOTTOM
OF POOL
ELEVATION
+ 309' -8"

7

118

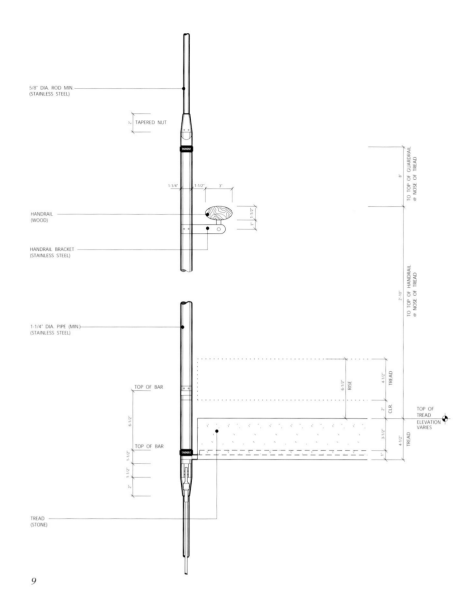

5/8" DIA. ROD MIN.
(STAINLESS STEEL)

TAPERED NUT

1-1/4" 1-1/2" 3"

HANDRAIL
(WOOD)

1-1/2"

HANDRAIL BRACKET
(STAINLESS STEEL)

TO TOP OF GUARDRAIL
@ NOSE OF TREAD

TO TOP OF HANDRAIL
@ NOSE OF TREAD

1-1/4" DIA. PIPE (MIN.)
(STAINLESS STEEL)

TOP OF BAR

6-1/2"

TOP OF BAR

1-1/2"

6-1/2" RISE

4-1/2" TREAD

CLR

TOP OF
TREAD
ELEVATION
VARIES

3-1/2" TREAD

4-1/2"

TREAD
(STONE)

9

10

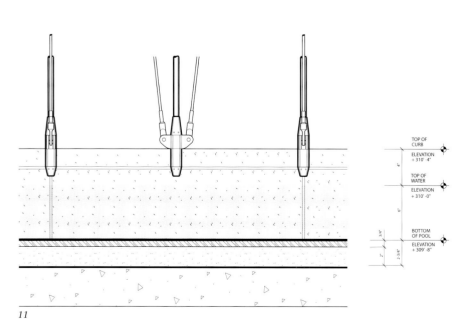

TOP OF
CURB
ELEVATION
+ 310'-4"

TOP OF
WATER
ELEVATION
+ 310'-0"

BOTTOM
OF POOL
ELEVATION
+ 309'-8"

11

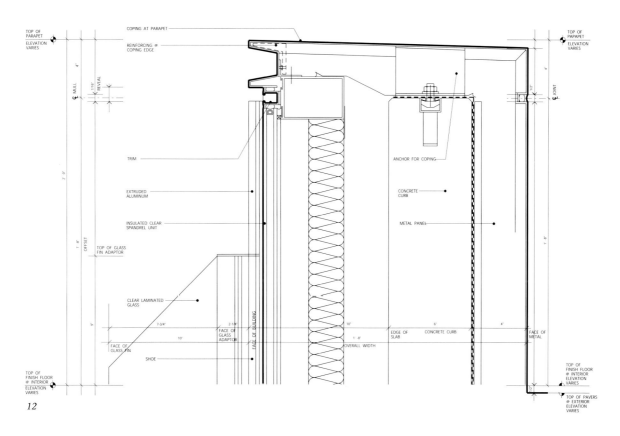

12

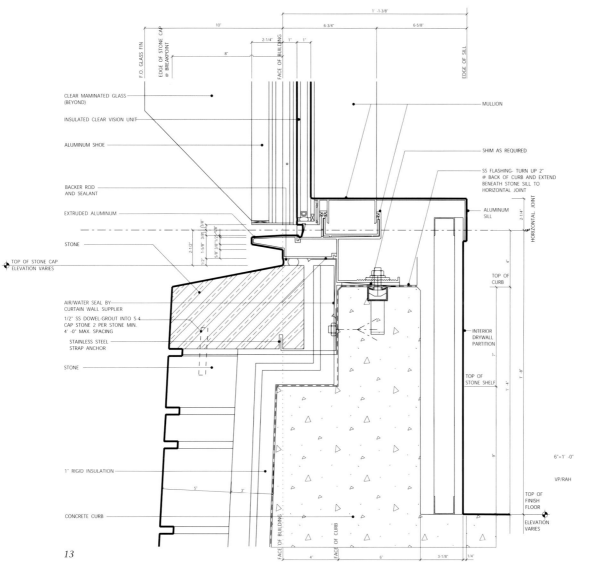

13

121

BRIDGE, CANOPY AND STAIR
ARMSTRONG RESIDENCE, POTOMAC, MARYLAND, USA
McInturff Architects

1

1 Entry façade
2 Entry bridge model
3 Axonometric of canopy support

This house for a couple with two grown children attempts to simplify the lives of the owners. It provides a small number of generous spaces in lieu of a larger number of particularised rooms.

Aside from requisite bedrooms, including one on the main level for future needs for accessibility, the program is reduced to an intimately scaled library, a generous, open kitchen and a large double-height room for living and dining.

This room takes the form of a half cylinder in order to gather in the views of the wooded site, while the remainder of the house fits within an orderly bar. The bar and the cylinder are then separated by a slot for light.

A landing at the top of the stairs occupies this slot and all circulation within the house involves moving between the two pieces. Materials – concrete, steel, glass and wood – are used in ways which express their natural properties.

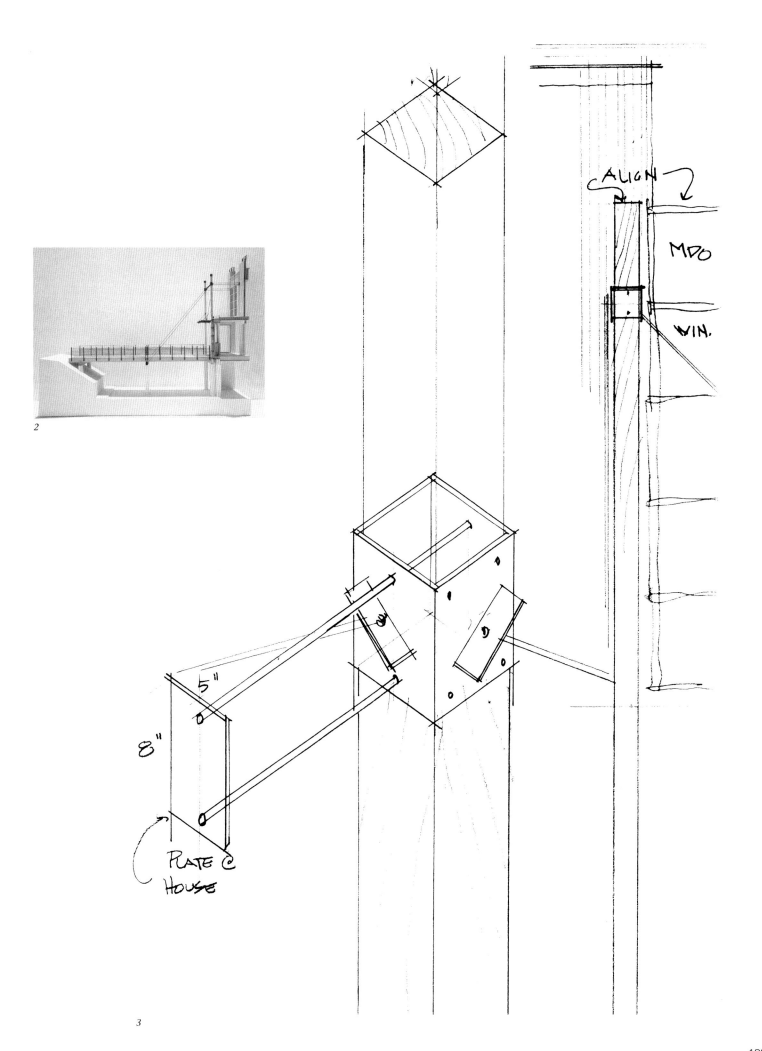

ALIGN

MDO

WIN.

5"

8"

PLATE @
HOUSE

4

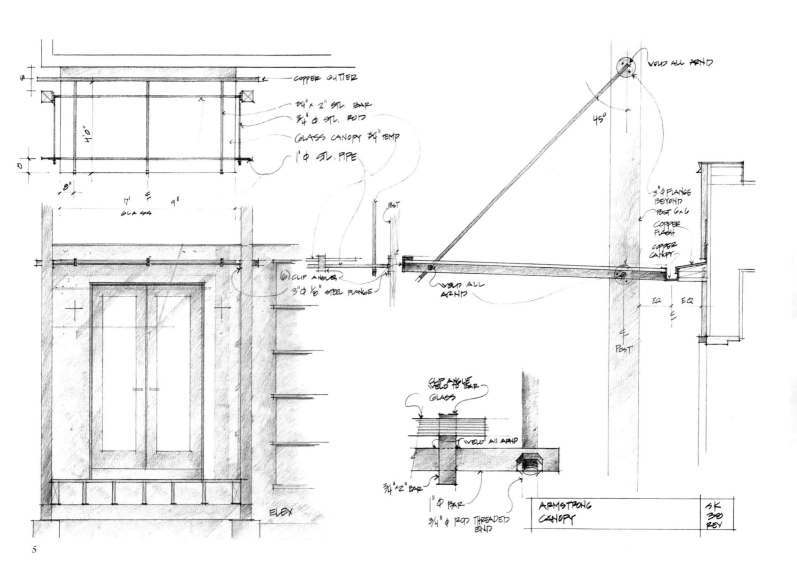

COPPER GUTTER

3/4" x 2" STL. BAR

3/4" Ø STL. ROD

GLASS CANOPY 3/4" TEMP

1" Ø STL. PIPE

4'0"

8"

1" & 9"
GLASS

(6) CLIP ANGLES
3" Ø 1/8" STEEL FLANGE

POST

WELD ALL ARND

45°

WELD ALL ARND

3" Ø FLANGE
BEYOND
POST 6x6
COPPER
FLASH
COPPER
CANOPY

EQ   EQ

& POST

ELEX

CLIP ANGLE
WELD TO BAR
GLASS

WELD ALL ARND

3/4" x 2" BAR

1" Ø BAR

3/4" Ø ROD THREADED
END

ARMSTRONG
CANOPY

SK
38
REY

5

125

6

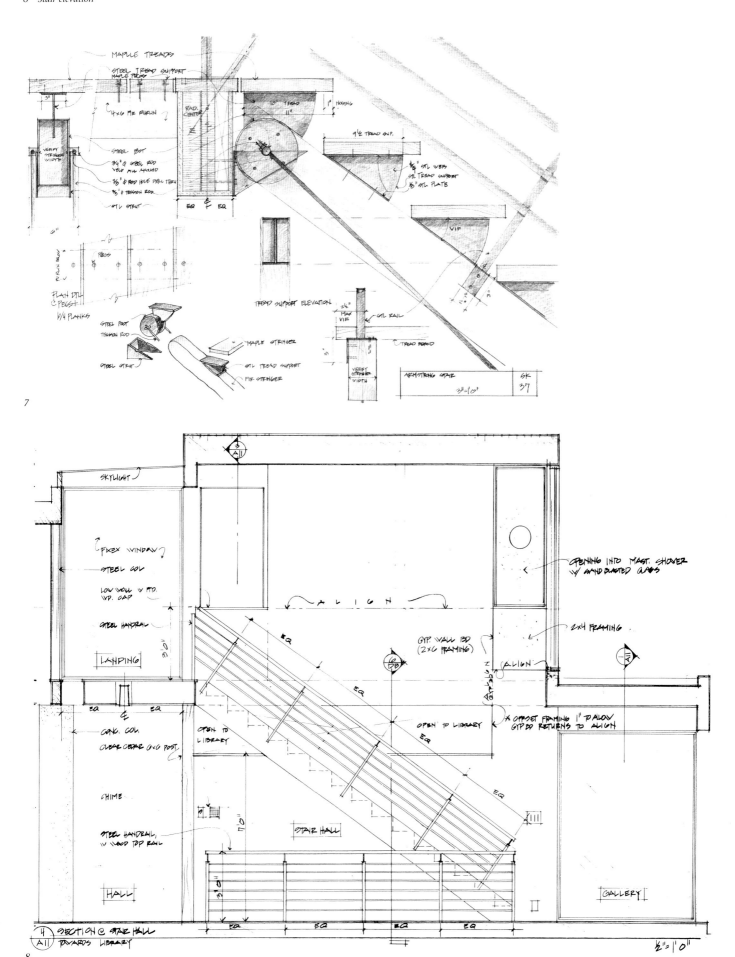

7

8

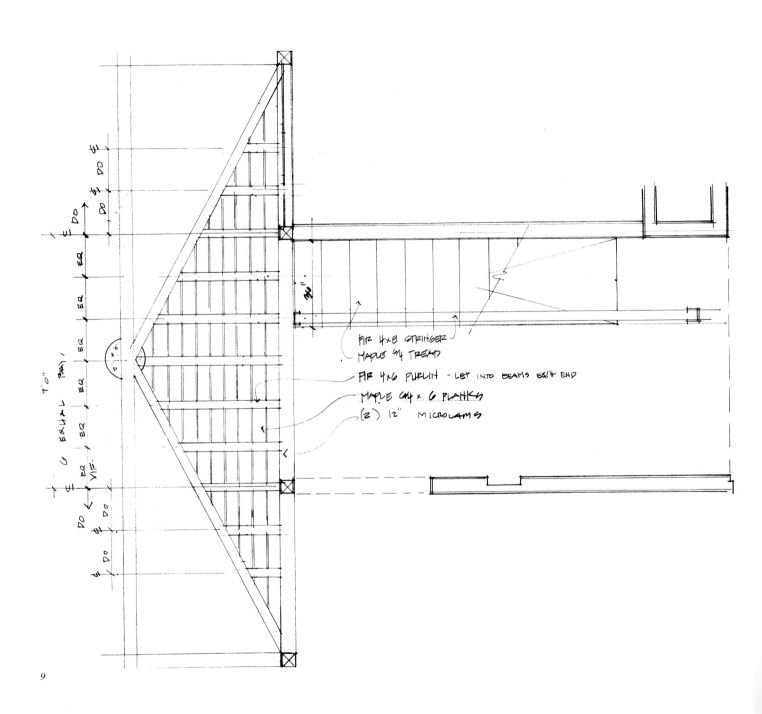

FIR 4x8 STRINGER
MAPLE 5/4 TREAD

FIR 4x6 PURLIN - LET INTO BEAMS EACH END

MAPLE 5/4 x 6 PLANKS

(2) 12" MICROLAMS

9

BRIDGE AND QUADRAPODS
WITHERS RESIDENCE, ACCOKEEK, MARYLAND, USA
McInturff Architects

1

2

1&2 *Metal and glass room bridging wings*
3 *Concept sketch*
4 *Axonometric*

This tiny house, designed for a professor of art history, occupies a wooded 10-acre site in rural southern Maryland. Its design process included the involvement of an astronomer making measurements one winter's solstice to ensure the perfect positioning of the house.

The client, who grew up in New England in a house designed by Dan Kiley, asked for two things – a simple cabin in the woods in the spirit of the Kiley house, and a proper setting for a commissioned Janet Saad Cook sun drawing.

The cabin exists in the two asphalt-shingled, tightly functional wings.

The Saad Cook structures are in the middle in a metal and glass room that bridges the wings. This space, which also houses the living and dining areas, is designed around this piece. Here the sun drawing projects reflected images, which change with the movement of the sun and clouds onto a wall to create an ephemeral response to place, time and architecture.

The glass wall is to the north, and the second-storey bridge that connects the two wings runs in front of it. This allows the south wall to receive the projected image on a billboard-like surface, which itself allows south light in only at the floor and ceiling.

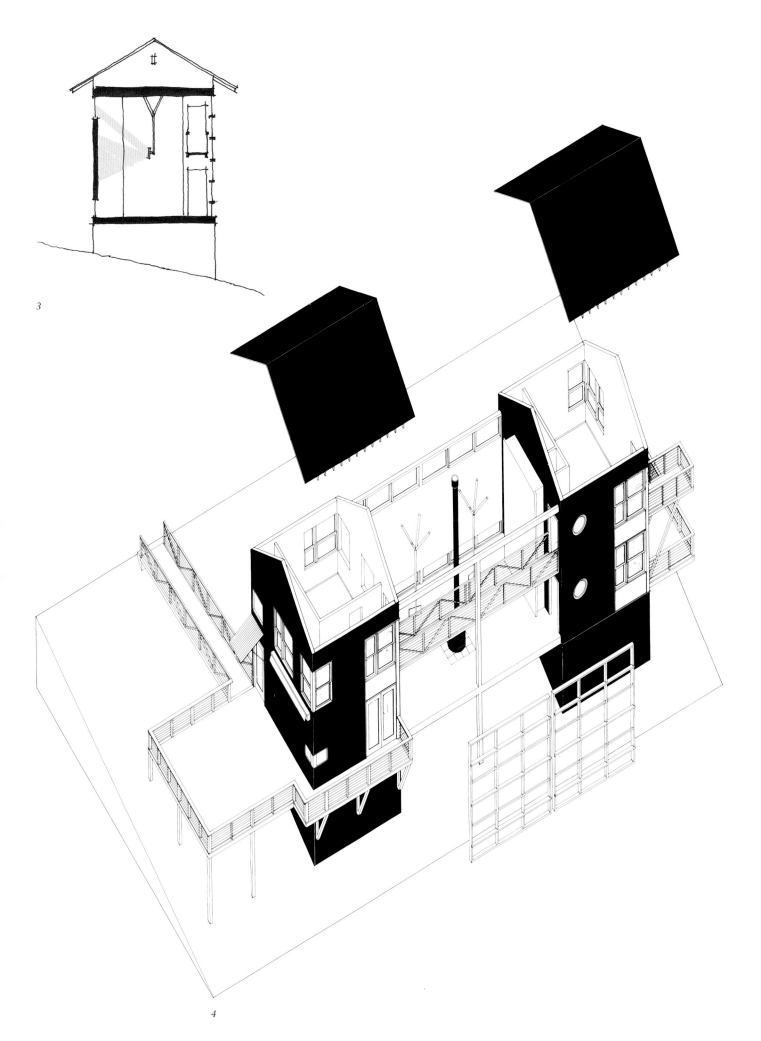

3

4

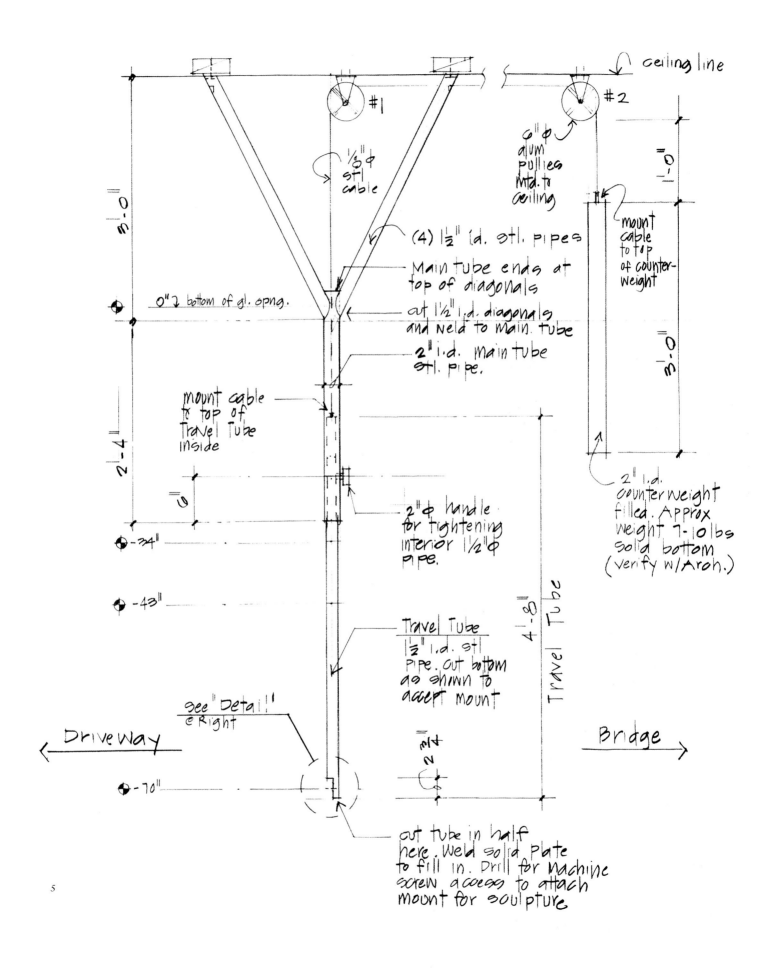

ceiling line

#1

#2

$\frac{1}{8}"\phi$
stl.
cable

6"ϕ
alum
pulleys
mtd. to
ceiling

mount
cable
to top
of counter-
weight

(4) $1\frac{1}{2}"$ i.d. stl. pipes

Main tube ends at
top of diagonals

0"∠ bottom of gl. opng.

at $1\frac{1}{2}"$ i.d. diagonals
and weld to main tube

2" i.d. main tube
stl. pipe.

mount cable
to top of
Travel Tube
inside

2"ϕ handle
for tightening
interior $1\frac{1}{2}"\phi$
pipe.

2" i.d.
counterweight
filled. Approx
weight 7-10 lbs
solid bottom
(verify w/Arch.)

–34"

–43"

Travel Tube
$1\frac{1}{2}"$ i.d. stl
pipe. cut bottom
as shown to
accept mount

Travel Tube

See "Detail"
@ Right

Driveway

Bridge

–70"

cut tube in half
here. Weld solid plate
to fill in. Drill for machine
screw access to attach
mount for sculpture

5

5   Elevation
6   Metal and glass room bridging wings
7   Housing especially designed for Janet Saad Cook work
Photography: Julia Heine

6

7

BUILT-IN BED
WEINER RESIDENCE, CAPITOL HILL, WASHINGTON DC, USA
McInturff Architects

1

*1&2 Bed cave beneath suspended wooden
      platform
   3 Model showing suspended platform
      and bed cave*

This renovation provided a rare opportunity to join two adjacent Capitol Hill alley houses, former workers' houses traditionally located behind larger city row houses. The client had occupied one alley house for more than a decade, and purchased the property next door.

One of the houses was gutted. New openings in the former party wall connect the two buildings. The bright, open new volume contains a stepped and suspended wooden platform that provides additional built-in seating adjacent to the existing second-floor living room.

A cave-like bed space below this platform functions as the new master bedroom, which is served by a bath in the existing house.

Fir beams of 13x18 centimetres span between the party walls and are pocketed into the brick. The elevations of the beams rise and fall to create seating platforms and steps.

Fir boards span the beams, with 6.4-millimetre gaps between boards to allow light and views to penetrate through the floor and heighten the perception of the platform as floating.

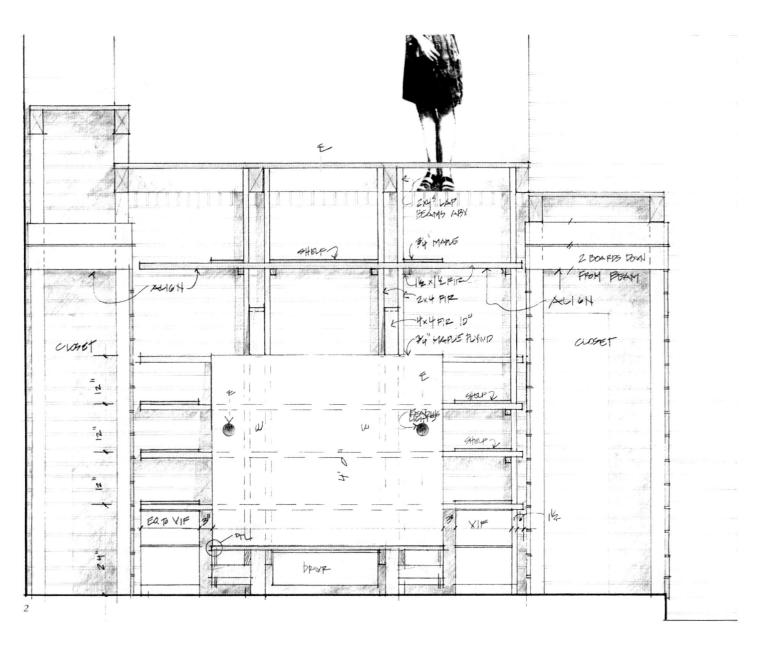

Within the drawing, handwritten annotations include:

E

2x9⁵ LAP
BEAMS ABX

¾" MAPLE

SHELF

2 BOARDS DOWN
FROM BEAM

1½ x 1½ FIR

2x4 FIR

ALIGN

4x4 FIR 10°

¾" MAPLE PLYWD

ALIGN

CLOSET

CLOSET

12"

12"

12"

24"

SHELF

READING
LIGHTS

SHELF

E

EQ TO VIF   3"

3"   VIF   1½

DRWR

2

Posts drop beneath the beams to sponsor closets,
shelves and a bed, and it becomes, intentionally,
unclear as to whether this is a large piece of
furniture or a small piece of building.

3

4   *Platform edge*
5   *Plan of bed*
6   *Axonometric of bed and closet structure*
7   *Side elevation of bed*
Opposite:
    Bed area with seating platform above
Photography: Julia Heine

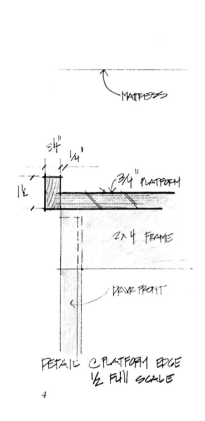

DETAIL @ PLATFORM EDGE
½ FULL SCALE

4

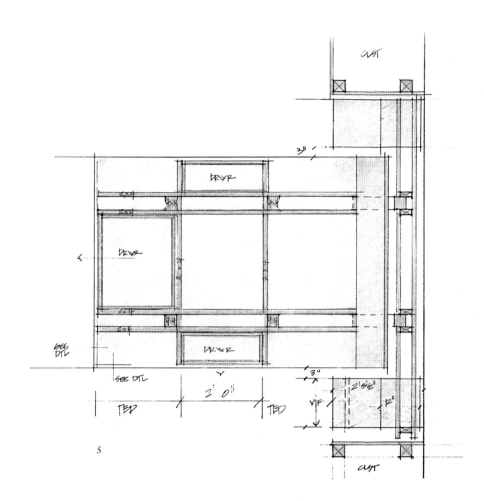

5

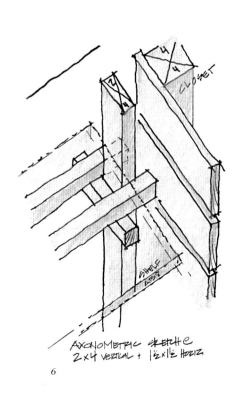

AXONOMETRIC SKETCH
2×4 VERTICAL + 1½×1½ HORIZ

6

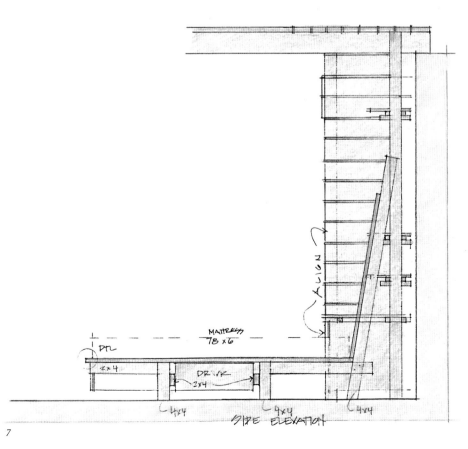

SIDE ELEVATION

7

READING ROOM PENDANT LIGHT FIXTURE
HUGH AND HAZEL DARLING LAW LIBRARY, UNIVERSITY OF CALIFORNIA, LOS ANGELES, CALIFORNIA USA
Moore Ruble Yudell Architects & Planners

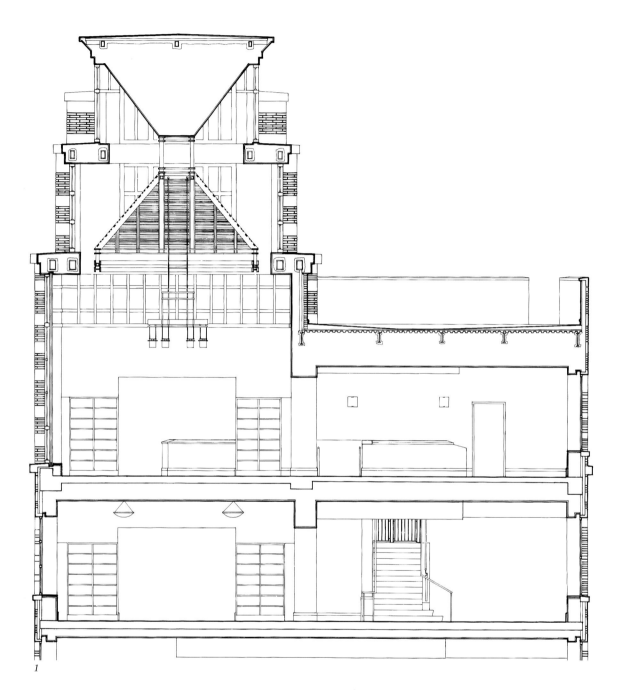

1

1   Section of reading room
2   Tower reading room

The fourth-floor reading room was designed as the 'crown' of the library tower. The tower establishes a strong image for the library, as well as an eastern end for the original axis of the UCLA campus.

The wood slat ceiling and custom pendant fixture create a light-filled spatially dynamic interior. The fixture, like the wood lattice interior ceiling, is open and transparent.

The painted aluminium pendant fixture utilises several different light sources to provide the light needed for the reading room.

Energy efficient and long-life compact fluorescent lamps, with amber glass diffusers, provide the ambient glow in the centre, and wash the wood lattice ceiling above.

Downlights are concealed within the structure of the chandelier to provide task lighting to the reading tables below.

2

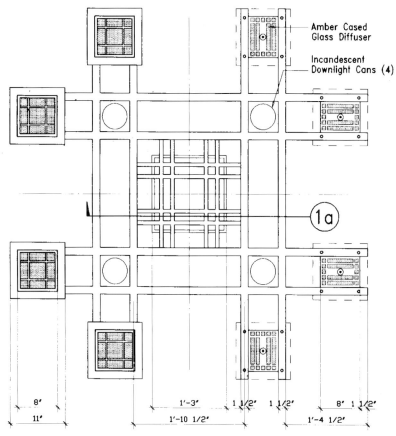

Amber Cased
Glass Diffuser

Incandescent
Downlight Cans (4)

1a

8' 11' 1'-3' 1 1/2' 1 1/2' 8' 1 1/2'
1'-10 1/2' 1'-4 1/2'

3

3   Plan from below
4   Detail section
5   Tower reading room pendant light fixture
6   Elevation
7   Detail section
8   Elevation and section of lantern
9   Ceiling plan of tower
Photography: Timothy Hursley

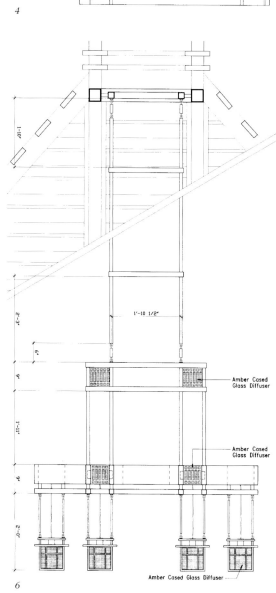

Amber Cased Glass Diffuser

Ballasts

Clear Acrylic Cover

(4) 18w Biax
Flourescent Lamps

4

5

Amber Cased
Glass Diffuser

Amber Cased
Glass Diffuser

1'-10 1/2'

Amber Cased Glass Diffuser

6

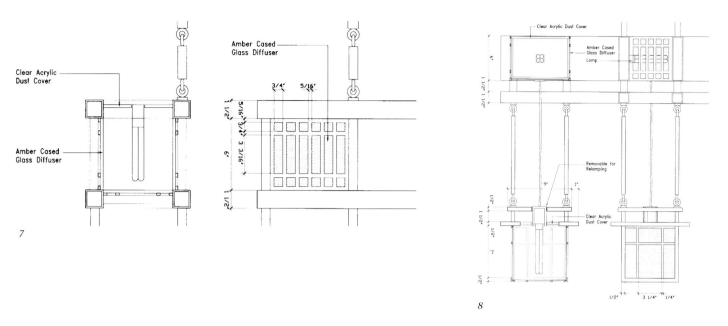

Clear Acrylic
Dust Cover

Amber Cased
Glass Diffuser

Amber Cased
Glass Diffuser

7

Clear Acrylic Dust Cover

Amber Cased
Glass Diffuser

Lamp

Removable for
Relamping

Clear Acrylic
Dust Cover

8

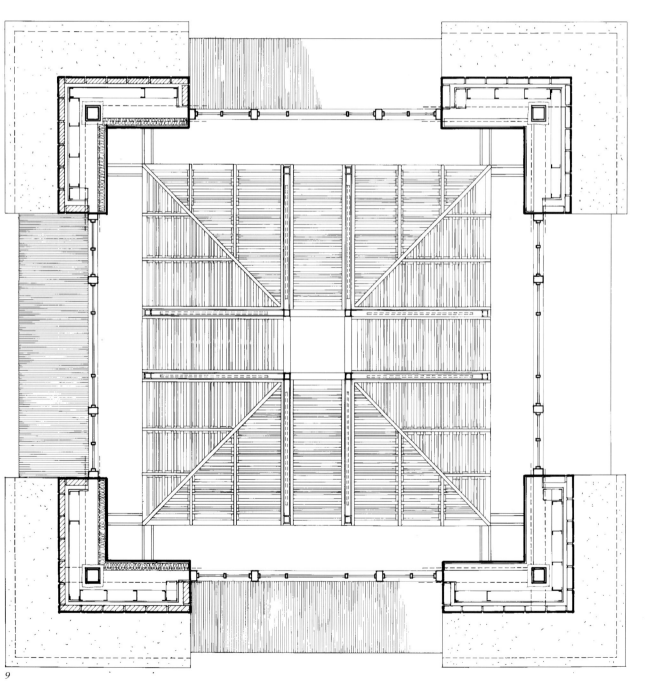

9

ENTRY DOOR
BLACKBURN RESIDENCE, GAINESVILLE, FLORIDA, USA
William Morgan Architects

1

2

3

Located on an exceptionally beautiful site, the Blackburn Residence is partially recessed into the gentle hilltop of a small peninsula between two lakes.

Approaching the residence from the west, visitors arrive in an informal entry court defined by the carport to the right, an elevated pond directly ahead, and a small masonry tower to the left flanking the front door.

The portal consists of 25 clear glass panes, each about 15 centimetres square, set into stout oak frames measuring overall approximately 183x203 centimetres.

Although from a distance the entry plane seems to be a single surface, an understated door handle marks the edge of the door that swings inward between two fixed side panels. Reveals rabbeted into the faces of the frames conceal the door jambs. An exterior keylock with interior deadbolt, similar in size and finish to the door bolts and washers, provide security.

Constructed on site by finish carpenters, the door frames are notched so that their surfaces are flush when they are assembled. Rabbeted frame edges receive glass panes during the assembly.

1   Sunlight streams through door into foyer
2   Fixed side panels flank swinging door
3   Entry court view at dusk
4   Elevation
5   Section
6   Entry drive approaching residence from west
Photography: F Wetterquist (1,2);
George Cott Chroma Inc (3,6)

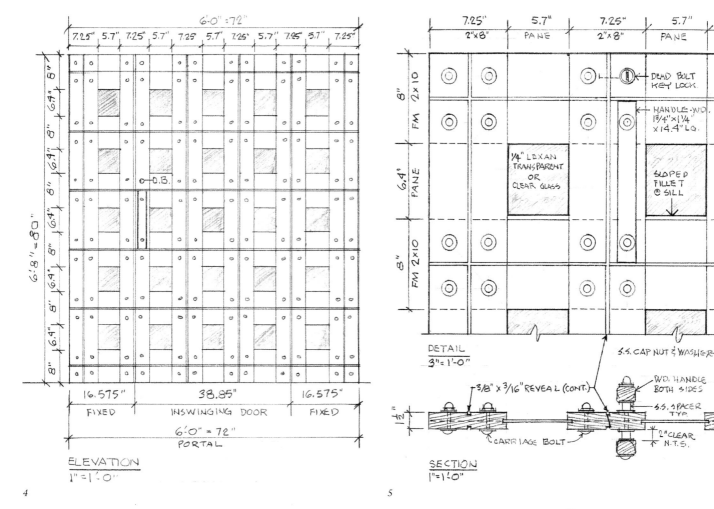

ELEVATION
1"=1'-0"

4

SECTION
1"=1'-0"

5

Four stainless steel bolts and washers calibrate each joint of the frame; their purpose is primarily ornamental although they also hold the wood frame members in place while glued joints cure.

The design is inspired in part by Lorenzo Ghiberti's beautiful bronze doors (1403–52) for the Bapistry of the Duomo in Florence, Italy.

6

CURTAINWALL, SKYLIGHT, BAMBOO ISLAND AND CURVED WALL

ORIENTAL PLAZA, BEIJING, PRC
P&T Group

1

1   Exterior of Oriental Plaza
2&3 Plaza skylight
4   Plaza skylight plan, section and
     elevation

This landmark development is a significant contribution to contemporary Beijing. Located along Chang'An Avenue and Wangfujing, a short distance from Tiananmen Square, the project combines 600,000 square metres of first-class commercial space, which also includes a 600-room five-star hotel, serviced apartments and a major shopping centre. Three groups of buildings, ranging from 14–20 storeys, are arranged around raised central courtyards.

The rectangular plan reinforces the traditional city grid with entrances marking the new major axes.

The square and circular building elements are differentiated in pink granite and reflective glass, applying a contemporary interpretation of classical Chinese motifs.

2

3

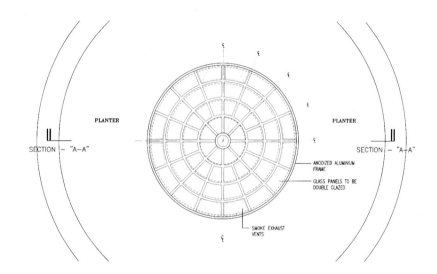

PLANTER

PLANTER

SECTION — "A—A"

SECTION — "A—A"

ANODIZED ALUMINIUM FRAME

GLASS PANELS TO BE DOUBLE GLAZED

SMOKE EXHAUST VENTS

PLAZA SKYLIGHT

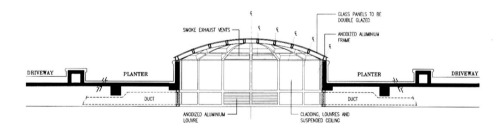

GLASS PANELS TO BE DOUBLE GLAZED

SMOKE EXHAUST VENTS

ANODIZED ALUMINIUM FRAME

DRIVEWAY

PLANTER

PLANTER

DRIVEWAY

DUCT

DUCT

ANODIZED ALUMINIUM LOUVRE

CLADDING, LOUVRES AND SUSPENDED CEILING

SECTION A—A

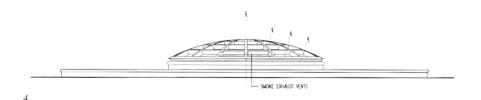

SMOKE EXHAUST VENTS

4

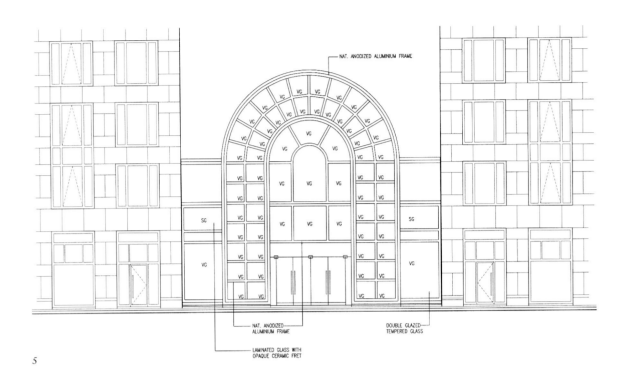

NAT. ANODIZED ALUMINIUM FRAME

NAT. ANODIZED ALUMINIUM FRAME

DOUBLE GLAZED TEMPERED GLASS

LAMINATED GLASS WITH OPAQUE CERAMIC FRET

5

6

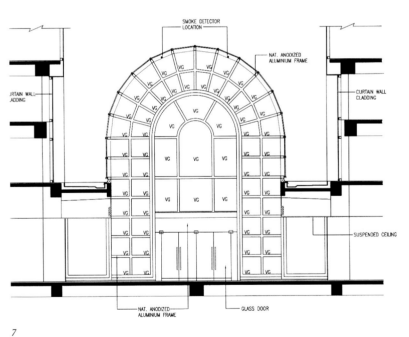

SMOKE DETECTOR LOCATION

NAT. ANODIZED ALUMINIUM FRAME

CURTAIN WALL CLADDING

CURTAIN WALL CLADDING

SUSPENDED CEILING

NAT. ANODIZED ALUMINIUM FRAME

GLASS DOOR

7

5 Elevation
6 Glass entrance of shopping arcade
7 Section
8 Section of glass entrance
9 Floor plan of glass entrance

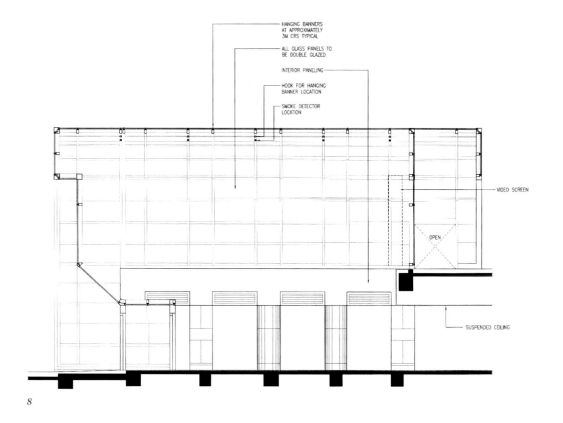

HANGING BANNERS
AT APPROXIMATELY
3M CRS TYPICAL

ALL GLASS PANELS TO
BE DOUBLE GLAZED

INTERIOR PANELING

HOOK FOR HANGING
BANNER LOCATION

SMOKE DETECTOR
LOCATION

VIDEO SCREEN

OPEN

SUSPENDED CEILING

8

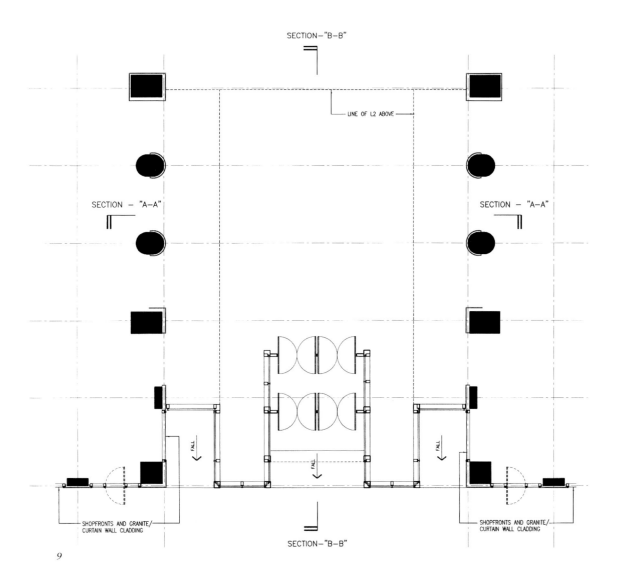

SECTION-"B-B"

LINE OF L2 ABOVE

SECTION - "A-A"

SECTION - "A-A"

FALL

FALL

FALL

SHOPFRONTS AND GRANITE/
CURTAIN WALL CLADDING

SHOPFRONTS AND GRANITE/
CURTAIN WALL CLADDING

SECTION-"B-B"

9

147

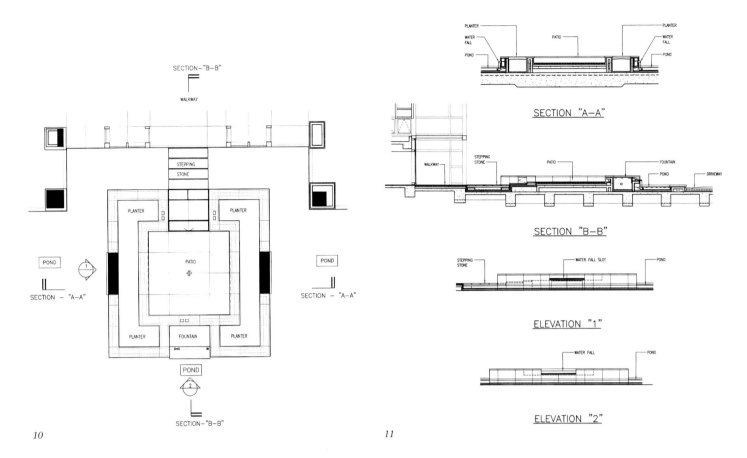

SECTION-"B-B"

WALKWAY

STEPPING

STONE

PLANTER   PLANTER

POND   PATIO   POND

1   SECTION - "A-A"   SECTION - "A-A"

PLANTER   FOUNTAIN   PLANTER

POND

2

SECTION-"B-B"

10

PLANTER   PATIO   PLANTER

WATER
FALL   WATER
FALL

POND   POND

SECTION "A-A"

STEPPING
STONE   PATIO   FOUNTAIN

WALKWAY   POND   DRIVEWAY

SECTION "B-B"

STEPPING
STONE   WATER FALL SLOT   POND

ELEVATION "1"

WATER FALL   POND

ELEVATION "2"

11

12

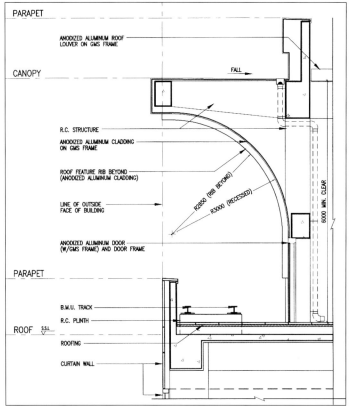

PARAPET

ANODIZED ALUMINUM ROOF
LOUVER ON GMS FRAME

CANOPY

FALL

R.C. STRUCTURE

ANODIZED ALUMINUM CLADDING
ON GMS FRAME

ROOF FEATURE RIB BEYOND
(ANODIZED ALUMINUM CLADDING)

LINE OF OUTSIDE
FACE OF BUILDING

R2850 (RIB BEYOND)
R3000 (RECESSED)

6000 MIN. CLEAR

ANODIZED ALUMINUM DOOR
(W/GMS FRAME) AND DOOR FRAME

PARAPET

B.M.U. TRACK
R.C. PLINTH

ROOF S.S.L

ROOFING

CURTAIN WALL

13

14

SKYLIGHT AND CURVED ROOF
HONG KONG MUSEUM OF HISTORY, HONG KONG, PRC
P&T Group

1

1 View of Museum of History building
2 Section across entrance lobby and exhibition area
3 Roof plan
4 Side façade
5 Aerial view

A museum development of 18,500 square metres, forming part of a museum complex, completes the master plan for the museums of science and history.

The main entrance draws visitors through an entrance piazza which has a view of the permanent exhibition area through a 13-metre-high glazed wall. The circulation was planned to provide clear independent access for general visitors, group visitors, staff and services.

An internal courtyard preserves certain mature trees on site and provides visual interest and spatial relief.

A grid of modular spaces comprised of 18 square metres, served by a 4.5 metre wide zone, gives clear circulation and access whilst providing maximum flexibility to the museum. The 18-square-metre space accommodates the exhibits, whilst the 4.5-metre freeze zone houses all the major services, routings, toilets and staircases. The modular grids are also expressed in the elevation treatment of the museum, especially on the façade facing the science museum.

A main feature of the development was the provision of a south-facing large open space as an external entrance foyer to both museums.

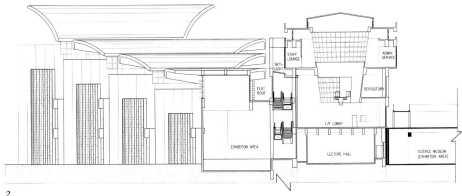

2

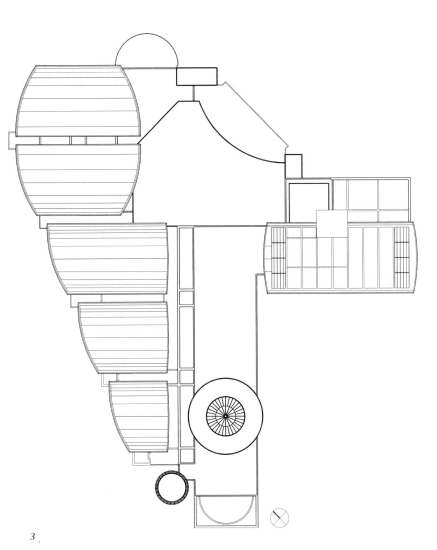

3

4

It is linked with the pedestrian system of the museum complex and pedestrian footbridges in the vicinity. Structural loading has been allowed for provision of externally located exhibits on the piazza.

The massing of the building volumes were carefully worked out in a stepped manner to provide a sense of scale along Chatham Road, and to produce the desired spatial quality inside the exhibition halls.

5

7

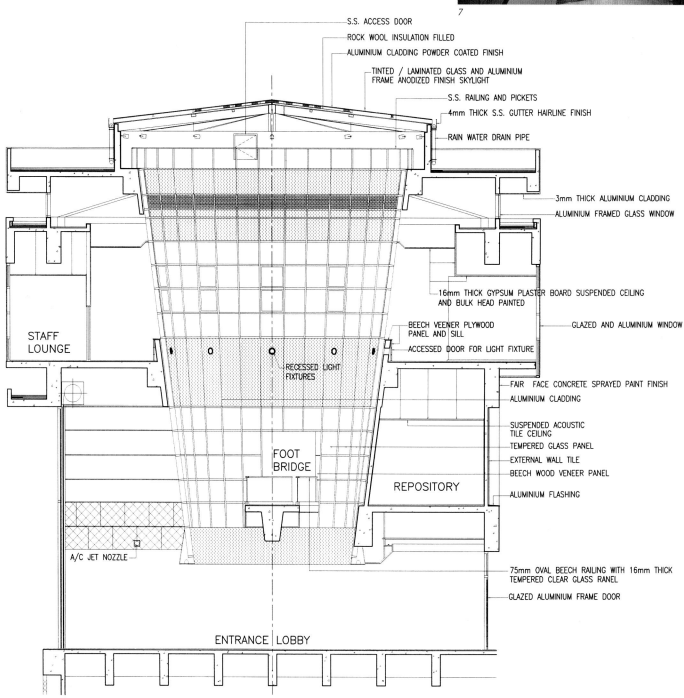

S.S. ACCESS DOOR

ROCK WOOL INSULATION FILLED

ALUMINIUM CLADDING POWDER COATED FINISH

TINTED / LAMINATED GLASS AND ALUMINIUM
FRAME ANODIZED FINISH SKYLIGHT

S.S. RAILING AND PICKETS

4mm THICK S.S. GUTTER HAIRLINE FINISH

RAIN WATER DRAIN PIPE

3mm THICK ALUMINIUM CLADDING

ALUMINIUM FRAMED GLASS WINDOW

16mm THICK GYPSUM PLASTER BOARD SUSPENDED CEILING
AND BULK HEAD PAINTED

GLAZED AND ALUMINIUM WINDOW

BEECH VEENER PLYWOOD
PANEL AND SILL

ACCESSED DOOR FOR LIGHT FIXTURE

FAIR FACE CONCRETE SPRAYED PAINT FINISH

ALUMINIUM CLADDING

SUSPENDED ACOUSTIC
TILE CEILING

TEMPERED GLASS PANEL

EXTERNAL WALL TILE

BEECH WOOD VENEER PANEL

ALUMINIUM FLASHING

75mm OVAL BEECH RAILING WITH 16mm THICK
TEMPERED CLEAR GLASS RANEL

GLAZED ALUMINIUM FRAME DOOR

STAFF
LOUNGE

RECESSED LIGHT
FIXTURES

FOOT
BRIDGE

REPOSITORY

A/C JET NOZZLE

ENTRANCE LOBBY

6

Photography: P&T Photographic Department

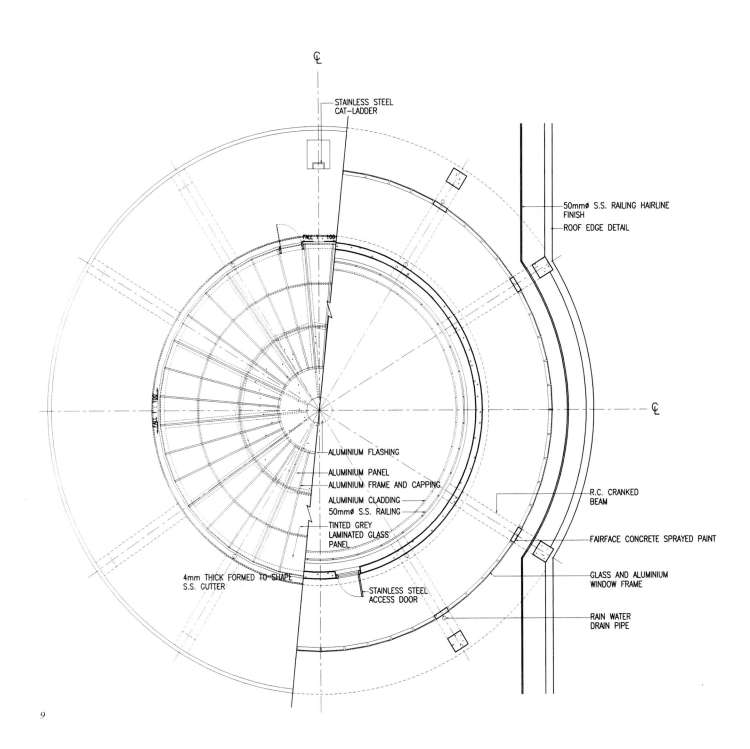

STAINLESS STEEL
CAT-LADDER

50mmø S.S. RAILING HAIRLINE
FINISH

ROOF EDGE DETAIL

ALUMINIUM FLASHING

ALUMINIUM PANEL

ALUMINIUM FRAME AND CAPPING

ALUMINIUM CLADDING

50mmø S.S. RAILING

TINTED GREY
LAMINATED GLASS
PANEL

4mm THICK FORMED TO SHAPE
S.S. GUTTER

STAINLESS STEEL
ACCESS DOOR

R.C. CRANKED
BEAM

FAIRFACE CONCRETE SPRAYED PAINT

GLASS AND ALUMINIUM
WINDOW FRAME

RAIN WATER
DRAIN PIPE

9

10

11

STRUCTURAL FRAME AND METAL SHEATHING
TFT/LCD PLANT, QUANTA DISPLAY INC., TAOYUAN COUNTY, TAIWAN
J.J. Pan and Partners Architects and Planners

1

1 *Transparency, reflection and shading in one of the courtyards*
2 *Cross section*

The program of the Quanta Display plan reflects the production of both liquid crystal display (LCD) and thin film transitory (TFT).

The selection of proven materials such as steel for the structural frame and metal sheathing provides an emphasis on the use of glass, thus symbolising the manufacture of LCD panels.

Glass not only forms a good part of the building envelope, it pulls away from the building in three places to evolve structurally as an entrance canopy and twin courtyard wall elements. The design

explores transparency and reflection as methods of dialogue between the building and its surroundings.

The glass is supported by a lightweight steel structural system coupled with pre-stressed steel cables. The result is a sense of fluidity against the massive fabrication structure that permits partial openings within the wall surface.

Round vertical posts reach 30 metres high; 26-centimetre steel tubes brace against wind pressure. Horizontal trusses capping the columns curve to

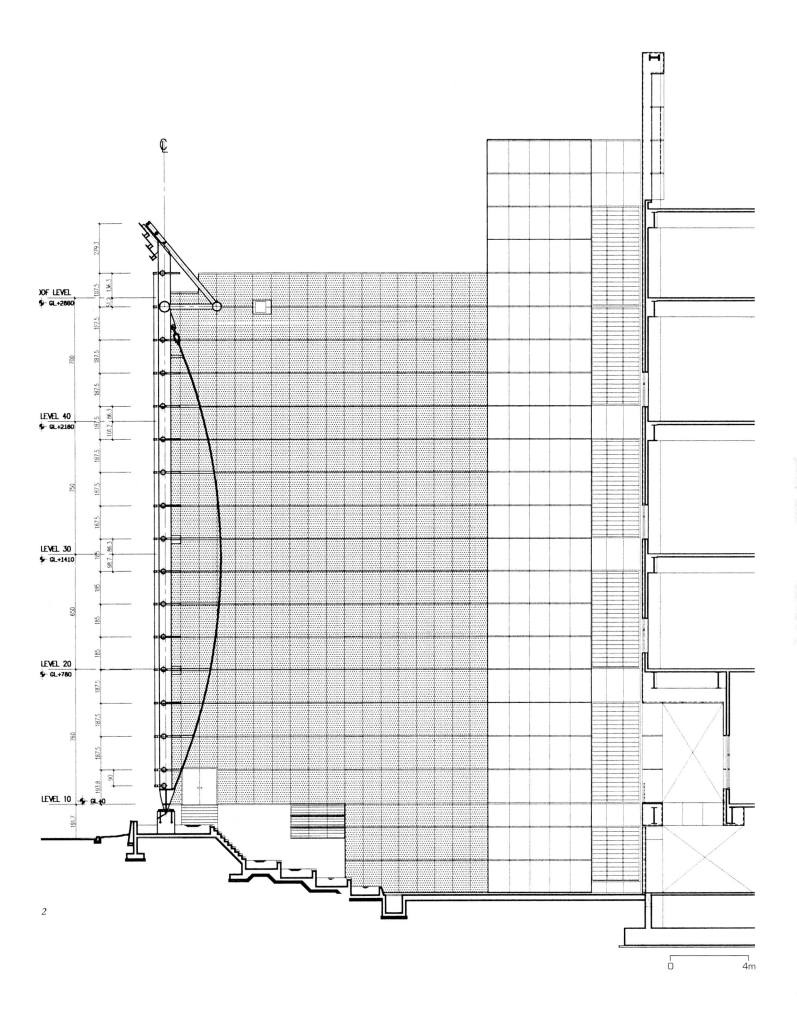

ROOF LEVEL
GL +2680

LEVEL 40
GL +2180

LEVEL 30
GL +1410

LEVEL 20
GL +780

LEVEL 10
GL ±0

2

0   4m

4

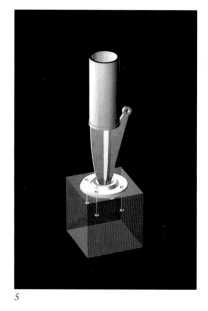

5

follow the main building façade, creating behind them a space of transition, lightness and a special sense of materiality.

The 70-metre entry canopy ellipse spans two structures, linked by an expansion joint. One end is fixed and the other cantilevered to allow for earthquake micro-movement.

6 Details
Opposite:
    Canopy structure
Photography: David Chen (1,3,8);
Jeffrey Cheng (4)

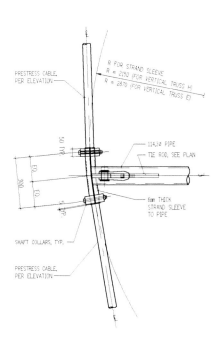

Pre-stress cable connection detail

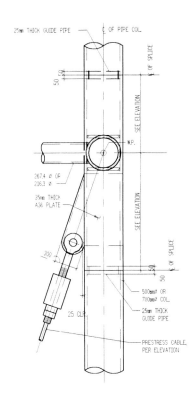

Bridge socket connection

6

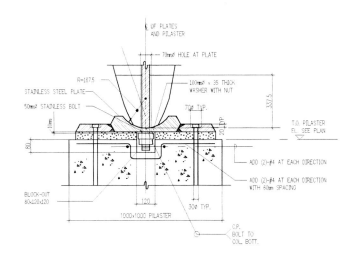

Steel column hinge support

0   0.5m

CURTAINWALL
EMBASSY SUITES, BATTERY PARK CITY, NEW YORK, NEW YORK, USA
Perkins Eastman Architects

1

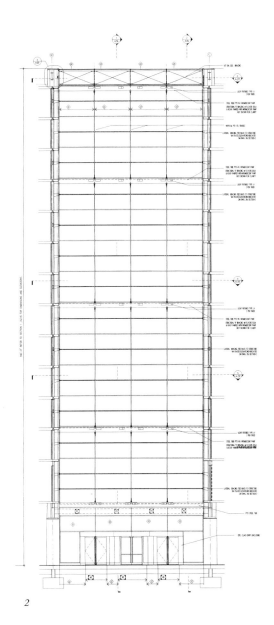

2

1   Exterior of 14-storey curtainwall atrium
2   Exterior elevation
Opposite:
    Interior of atrium space

The major design feature at the Embassy Suites Hotel in Battery Park City is the 14-storey atrium that sits between a narrow slab and a larger block of the building. The front façade of this atrium is a 43-metre-tall fully glazed curtainwall that overlooks the Hudson River.

Cost-efficient design was paramount in the client's mind for this project. Therefore, the design and detail of the wall were developed with an off-the-shelf curtainwall system attached to custom-designed steel trusses.

The trusses span the main lateral bracing connection between the two halves of the building. By visually integrating the curtainwall and superstructure, Perkins Eastman Architects was able to create a dynamic design that met the client's budget.

4 *Section of trusses*
Opposite:
  Interior of 43-metre-tall glass curtainwall

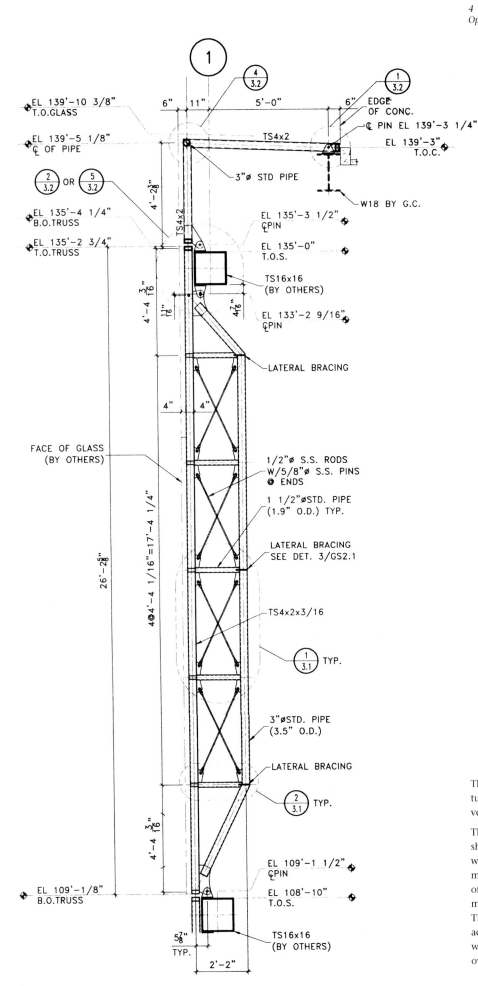

EL 139'-10 3/8"
T.O.GLASS

EL 139'-5 1/8"
℄ OF PIPE

② OR ⑤
3.2   3.2

EL 135'-4 1/4"
B.O.TRUSS

EL 135'-2 3/4"
T.O.TRUSS

FACE OF GLASS
(BY OTHERS)

26'-2 5/8"

6" 11" 5'-0" 6" EDGE
OF CONC.

①   ④   ①
3.2   3.2

TS4x2

3"⌀ STD PIPE

℄ PIN EL 139'-3 1/4"

EL 139'-3"
T.O.C.

W18 BY G.C.

EL 135'-3 1/2"
℄PIN

EL 135'-0"
T.O.S.

TS16x16
(BY OTHERS)

EL 133'-2 9/16"
℄PIN

LATERAL BRACING

1/2"⌀ S.S. RODS
W/5/8"⌀ S.S. PINS
@ ENDS

1 1/2"⌀STD. PIPE
(1.9" O.D.) TYP.

LATERAL BRACING
SEE DET. 3/GS2.1

TS4x2x3/16

① TYP.
3.1

3"⌀STD. PIPE
(3.5" O.D.)

LATERAL BRACING

② TYP.
3.1

EL 109'-1 1/2"
℄PIN

EL 108'-10"
T.O.S.

EL 109'-1/8"
B.O.TRUSS

TS16x16
(BY OTHERS)

5 7/8"
TYP.

2'-2"

4'-2 3/8"

4'-4 3/16"

4@4'-4 1/16"=17'-4 1/4"

4'-4 3/16"

The steel trusses are fabricated of painted steel tubing with stainless steel rod bracing, and are vertically approximately nine metres.

The clevis plates on the trusses were custom shaped to express the forces acting in the rods while minimising their mass. A unitised curtain mullion system was attached to the front chord of the trusses with small plates, further minimising the profile of the curtainwall system. The trusses were braced horizontally with rods across the back of the trusses. At the top of the wall the glass is returned; further lightening the overall effect of the wall.

6   *Detail where trusses join main lateral*
    bracing
7   *Main section showing pedestrian bridges,*
    main lateral bracing and glass curtainwall
8   *Plan of truss and glass wall assembly*
Opposite:
    Interior of 43-metre-tall glass curtainwall
Photography: Chuck Choi
Drawings: Perkins Eastman Architects and
Advanced Structures Incorporated

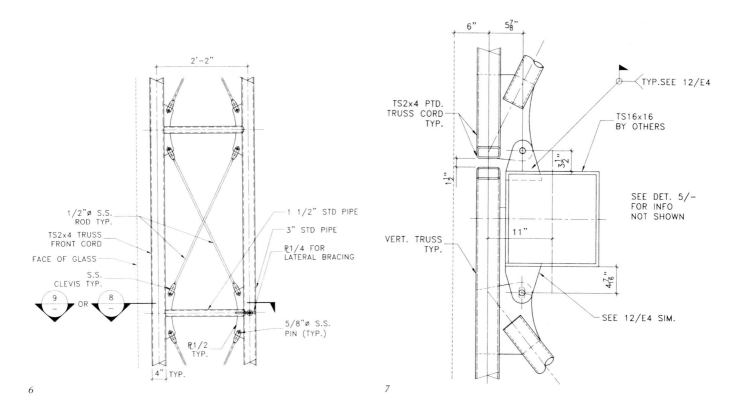

6

7

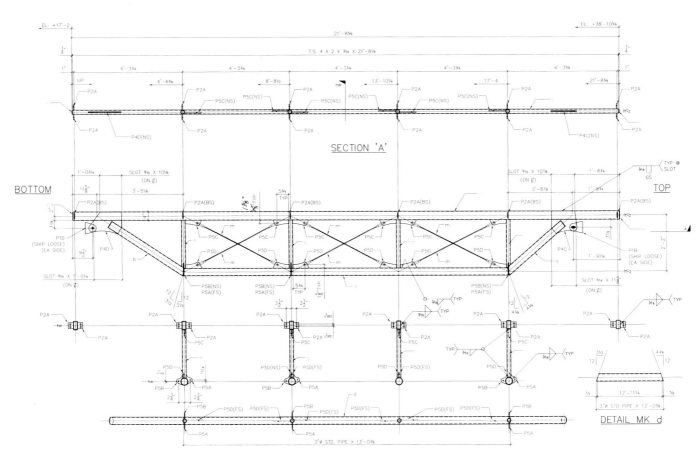

8

GLASS CANOPY
MARRIOTT EAST HOTEL, NEW YORK, NEW YORK, USA
Perkins Eastman Architects

1

1 *Front façade with glass canopy*
2 *Plan view*
3 *Front elevation*

The glass canopy at the Marriott East Hotel was part of a major renovation and image upgrade. The new canopy was designed around the recessed entrance colonnade in such a way as to enhance and preserve the existing limestone façade. With minimal building contact, the design utilises merely six anchoring points.

The canopy is comprised of six primary components: the painted white, 11-metre bow-shaped, steel arch superstructure; 13 double stainless steel fin plates; 2-centimetre tempered glass laminated with a 60 per cent ceramic frit; stainless steel catenary cables; and a stainless steel gutter.

The glass sheets are horizontally point suspended from the fins, which radiate from the arch superstructure. This bow-shaped piece is connected at each end by a round tube running along the back of the canopy and behind the existing columns, rests within two brackets and is slotted to allow the arch to be slid into position and enable precise on-site rotation.

The arch is suspended from an upper catenary cable, anchored at just two points on the façade with clevis plates custom designed to enable custom rotation.

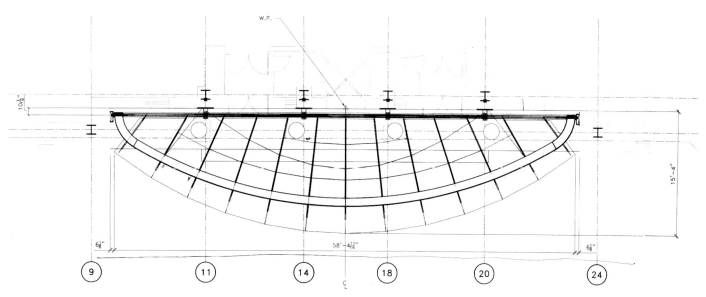

W.P.

$10\frac{1}{2}$"

$15'-4"$

$6\frac{1}{8}$" $58'-4\frac{11}{16}$" $6\frac{1}{8}$"

(9)   (11)   (14)   (18)   (20)   (24)

C̵L

2

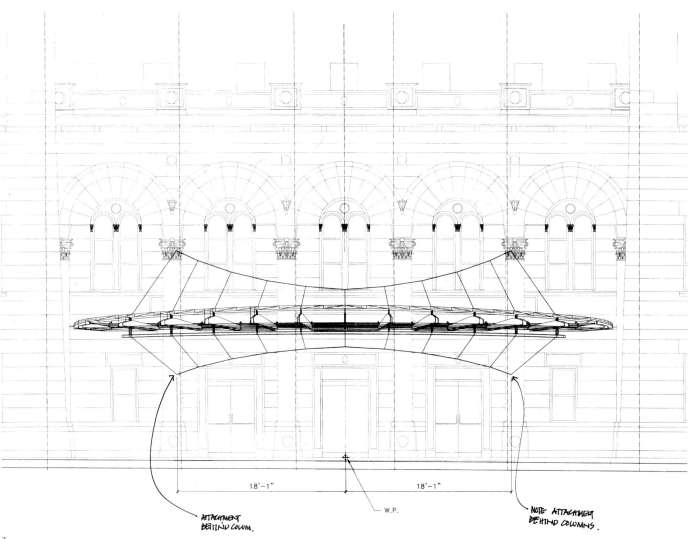

NOTE ATTACHMENT
BEHIND COLUMNS.

18'-1"   18'-1"

W.P.

ATTACHMENT
BEHIND COLUM.

NOTE ATTACHMENT
BEHIND COLUMNS.

3

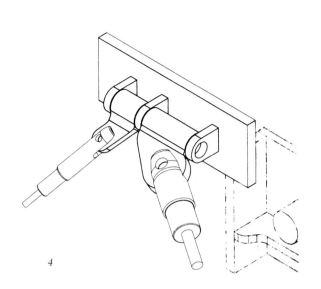

4

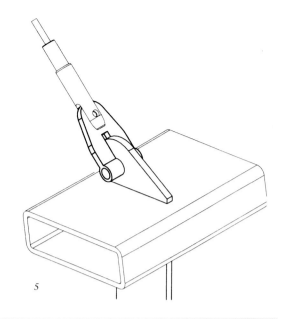

5

6

In order to counteract uplifting wind loads, a second catenary was required below the glass plane and anchored at the façade similar to above. The cables were attached to the main arch superstructure through a spreader plate suspended from the arch between the glass joints.

The whole structure is canted slightly to drain toward the gutter suspended from the back of the main arch support, close to the building.

7

4 Catenary cable wall anchor detail
5 Upper catenary cable and bow-shaped arch superstructure detail
6 Upper catenary cable anchor
7 Detail of stainless steel spreader plates
8 View showing fin plates, glass, spreader plates and catenary cables
Photography: Chuck Choi
Drawings: Perkins Eastman Architects and
Advanced Structures Incorporated

8

GLASS CURTAINWALL WITH STAINLESS STEEL SUPPORTING TRUSS

UNIVERSITY OF CONNECTICUT, STAMFORD, CONNECTICUT, USA

Perkins Eastman Architects

1

1   Exterior of academic concourse showing
    uninterrupted glass wrap corner
2   Interior of academic concourse
3   Custom-fabricated compression strut and
    solid nosing

The University of Connecticut's academic concourse is enclosed with a taut glass skin, point-supported on stainless steel catenary trusses. Affording the maximum level of transparency, the concourse enclosure comprises three major elements: bored, insulated glass; cast stainless steel 'spiders' with planar 915 bolts; and a custom-designed stainless steel supporting truss.

The dead load of the glass is transmitted vertically through the glass to the bottom of the wall where a rod transmits it back up to a supporting structure at the top of the wall. Wind loads are handled by the custom-designed trusses. Two catenaries, separated by compression struts, work

in tension, opposing one another, and therefore maintaining equilibrium. The trusses span approximately 18.3 metres between the cantilevered tube steel superstructure. Trussed columns were designed at the corners of the concourse, allowing the glass to wrap uninterrupted around the corner. To stabilise the trusses horizontally, tie rods were run through their centres.

Compression struts were fabricated from two parts: a shaft of 10-centimetre-diameter hollow stainless steel tubes with a solid nosing machined with a bolt hole for a 'spider' fitting and threaded attachments for the vertical dead load rods made

2

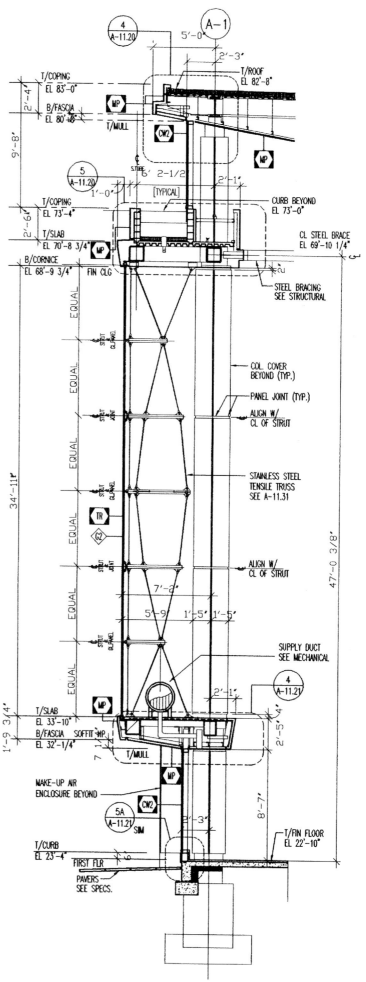

with cold-formed heads and attached with clevises to the plates on the struts. The struts were slotted to receive individually shaped plates and shop-welded in place to extenuate the direction of the forces acting through the plates. The ends of the hollow tube struts were finished with a stainless steel cap insert.

Great attention to detail was paid to each component and the success of the design, fabrication and installation of this truss wall was the result of a careful collaboration between Perkins Eastman Architects and Advanced Structures Incorporated.

3

173

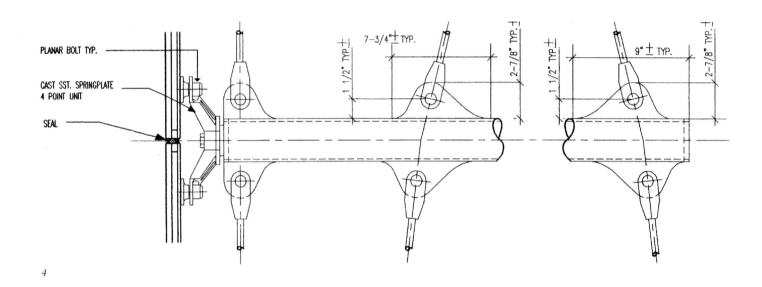

PLANAR BOLT TYP.

CAST SST. SPRINGPLATE
4 POINT UNIT

SEAL

7-3/4" ± TYP.

1 1/2" ± TYP.

2-7/8" TYP. ±

9" ± TYP.

1 1/2" ± TYP.

2-7/8" TYP. ±

4

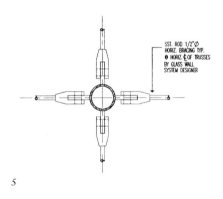

SST. ROD 1/2" Ø
HORIZ. BRACING TYP.
Ç HORIZ. Ç OF TRUSSES
BY GLASS WALL
SYSTEM DESIGNER

5

6

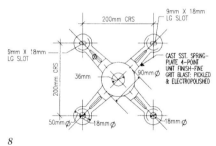

9mm X 18mm
LG SLOT

200mm CRS

9mm X 18mm
LG SLOT

200mm CRS

36mm

90mm

CAST SST. SPRING-
PLATE 4-POINT
UNIT FINISH-FINE
GRIT BLAST: PICKLED
& ELECTROPOLISHED

50mm Ø

18mm Ø

18mm Ø

8

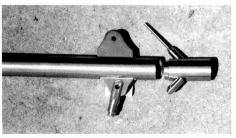

7

4   *Strut detail*
5   *Section of strut detail*
6&7 *Complex strut assembly*
8   *'Spider' detail*
Opposite:
   *Detail of custom-designed catenary
   truss and glass wall system*
Photography: Chuck Choi
*Drawings: Perkins Eastman Architects and
Advanced Structures Incorporated*

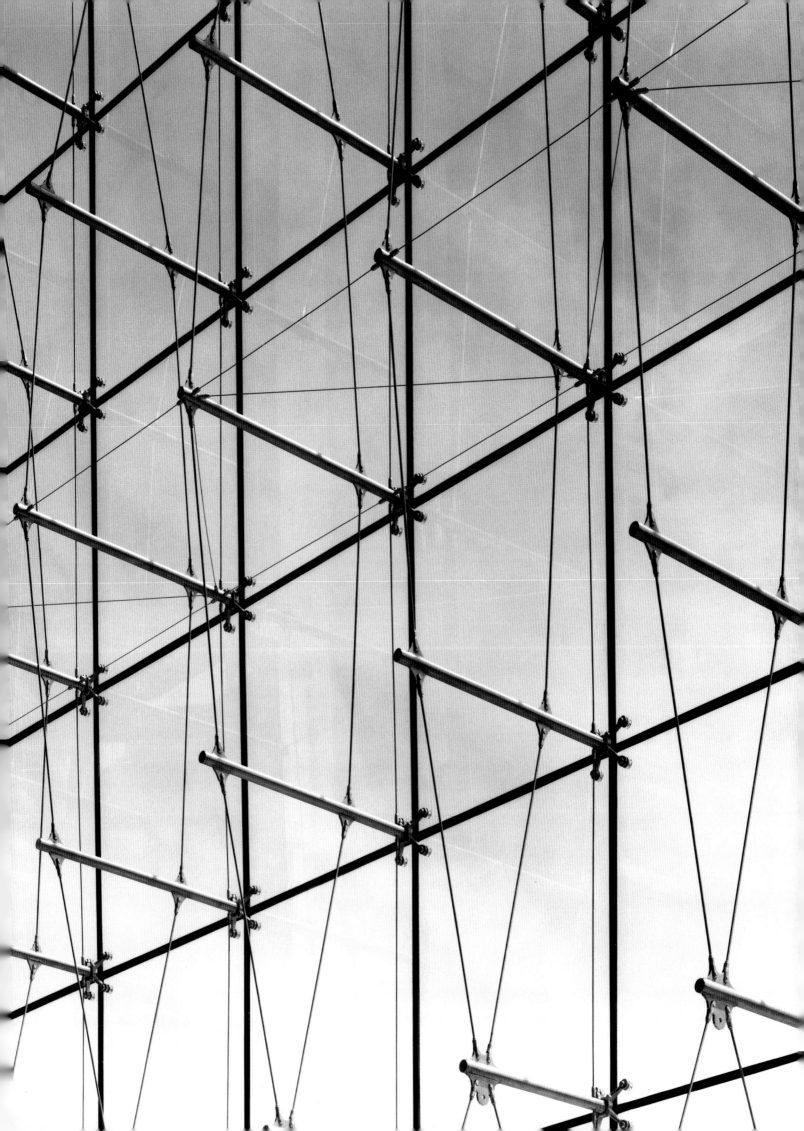

VIVARIUM
MUSEUM OF NATURAL HISTORY, BUTTERFLY VIVARIUM, NEW YORK, NEW YORK, USA
Perkins Eastman Architects

1

Perkins Eastman collaborated with the museum's exhibition department in the design of the butterfly vivarium, a custom-fabricated shell structure within one of the museum's existing galleries. It is a completely self-contained sub-tropical environment for the exhibition of live butterflies.

Constructed of translucent Kalwall panels, transparent acrylic panels, aluminium panels and c-channels, the vivarium is designed as a lightweight 402-square-metre shell-type 'kit of parts' that can be erected and dismantled seasonally.

The structure is divided into two zones, an enclosed 'flight' space and an open 'queuing' corridor. Visitors first experience the queuing corridor where aluminium columns support Kalwall ceiling panels, which span the enclosed flight space and arc into the opposite supporting wall. The columns are integrated with the information graphics and vitrines. To the viewer's left, transparent acrylic panels separate the corridor from the enclosed flight space. At the short ends, entry and exit vestibules are made of aluminium honeycomb panels.

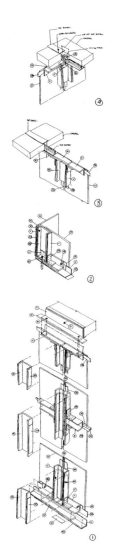

2

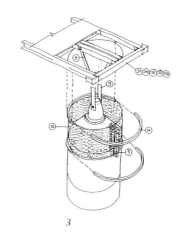

3

1   Interior flight space
2   Joint assembly
3   Custom-designed halide lamp
4   Queuing corridor looking into flight space
Photography: C.Chesek (1); Perkins Eastman
Architects and Advanced Structures Incorporated
(2); Perkins Eastman Architects (3&4)

Inside the flight space, spanning between the
Kalwall ceiling panels, is a series of service panels
to accommodate all lighting, and supply and
return air outlets. Custom-designed halide lamps
focus light onto planted landscaping while the
heat from these fixtures is exhausted into the
return air system. Maintained by its own HVAC
system, supply and return air is fed to the space
via galvanised steel ductwork on top of the
structure. The flooring is completely sealed, with
recycled rubber sheet adhered to the existing
terrazzo floor.

4

DINING TABLE
3905 CLAY STREET, SAN FRANCISCO, CALIFORNIA, USA
Pfau Architecture Ltd.

1

The project consists of an interior remodel of a 1906 nondescript four-storey brown shingle home, that has been parcelled into two properties in the early 1970s. The challenge was to create a 'transformative interior', while keeping exterior changes to a minimum.

The architect positioned dining at the centre, making dining, living and kitchen function as one space. New interior walls were treated as furniture, with kitchen cabinets and casework materials embedded into plaster and stud wall construction.

The dining table was integrated into the new interior design as the centrepiece of the remodel: elegant, understated and deceptively simple.

Steel friction-fit pins and removable leaf ends allow the teak and stainless steel table to seat from six to ten persons. The continuous frame is welded and polished. Teak boards are biscuit joined and oil finished.

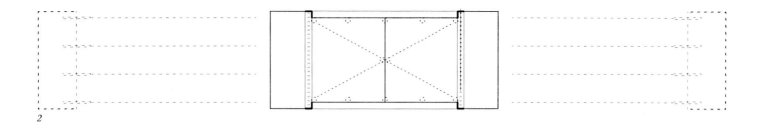

2

3

1   Dining table detail
2   Dining table for six to ten people
3   Diagrammatic sketch
4   Dining/living area
Photography: Cesar Rubio

4

ENTRY LOBBY
APARTMENT BUILDING, ELIZABETH BAY, NEW SOUTH WALES, AUSTRALIA
Rihs Architects (Gerry Rihs + Sergio Melo e Azevedo)

1

1   *Three-dimensional modelling of entry lobby*
2   *Balcony detail*
3   *Entry lobby initial sketch*

The sculptural concrete volumes, which identify the building, established the level of design and image that Rihs Architects wanted to carry throughout the project.

The building entrance is defined by a double-height glazed wall with a dynamic canopy.

Both are made of steel channels and laminated safety glass. The curved canopy is pitched to the sky and made with two glass panels. It creates a sharp edge like a blade that juts from the building. The glass fixture was designed to allow the glass to float over the steel structure.

Internally, the glass wall, which defines the entrance, is returned along the carpark with floodlights behind it to create a warm ambience at night. A small balcony at the end of the lobby permits access to the first-floor carpark. The concrete balcony is very similar in shape to the glass canopy.

Once again the curved edge reinforced by a steel channel creates a sharp edge which cuts through space in an elegant manner. The balcony blades are of aluminium, and shaped to resemble the concrete sails of the building façade.

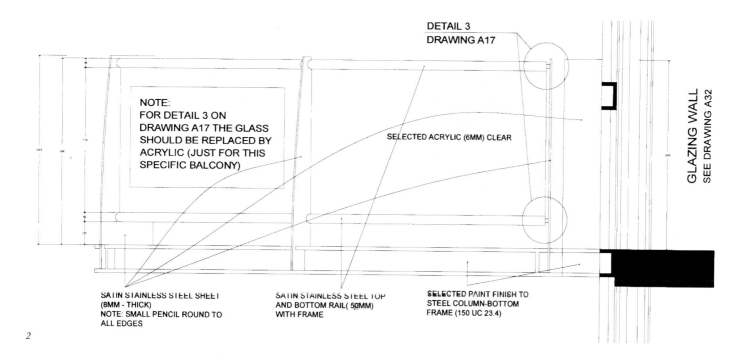

NOTE:
FOR DETAIL 3 ON
DRAWING A17 THE GLASS
SHOULD BE REPLACED BY
ACRYLIC (JUST FOR THIS
SPECIFIC BALCONY)

DETAIL 3
DRAWING A17

SELECTED ACRYLIC (6MM) CLEAR

GLAZING WALL
SEE DRAWING A32

SATIN STAINLESS STEEL SHEET
(8MM - THICK)
NOTE: SMALL PENCIL ROUND TO
ALL EDGES

SATIN STAINLESS STEEL TOP
AND BOTTOM RAIL(50MM)
WITH FRAME

SELECTED PAINT FINISH TO
STEEL COLUMN-BOTTOM
FRAME (150 UC 23.4)

2

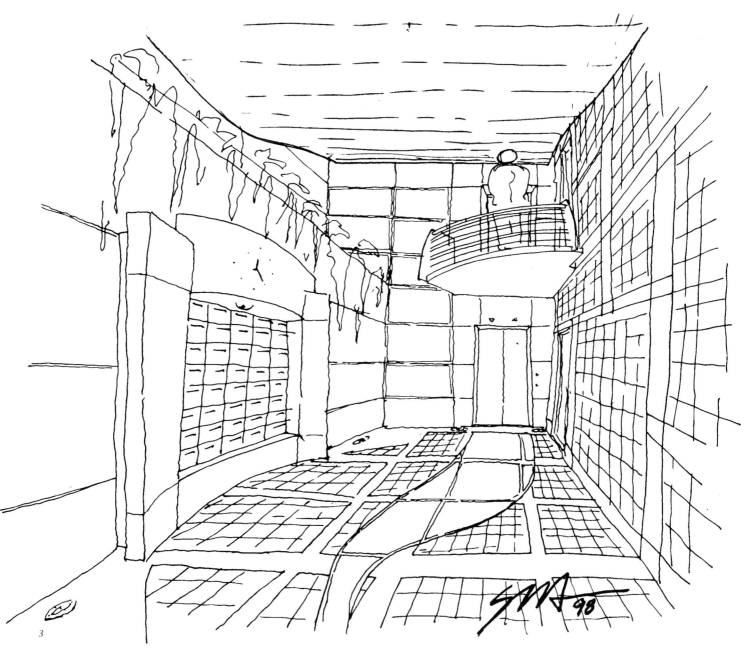

3

181

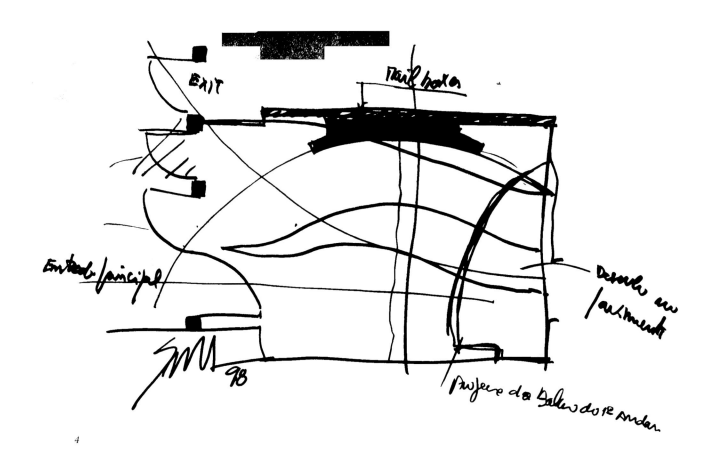

EXIT

Mail boxes

Entrada Principal

Descer ao pavimento

Projeto da Galeria do 1º Andar

98

4

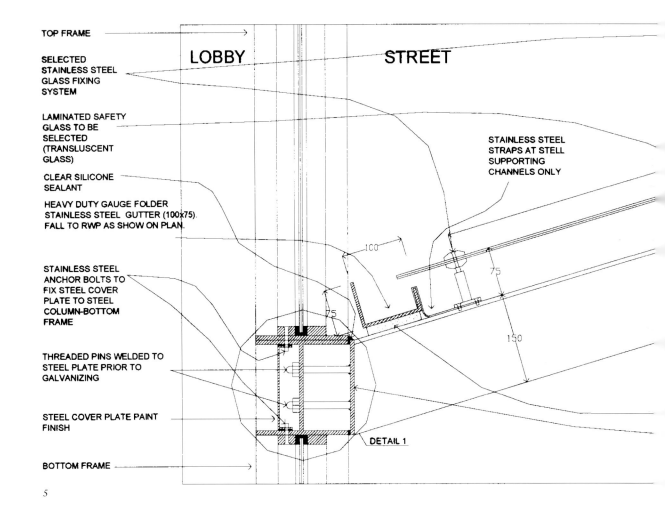

TOP FRAME

LOBBY   STREET

SELECTED
STAINLESS STEEL
GLASS FIXING
SYSTEM

LAMINATED SAFETY
GLASS TO BE
SELECTED
(TRANSLUSCENT
GLASS)

STAINLESS STEEL
STRAPS AT STELL
SUPPORTING
CHANNELS ONLY

CLEAR SILICONE
SEALANT

HEAVY DUTY GAUGE FOLDER
STAINLESS STEEL GUTTER (100x75).
FALL TO RWP AS SHOW ON PLAN.

100

75

STAINLESS STEEL
ANCHOR BOLTS TO
FIX STEEL COVER
PLATE TO STEEL
COLUMN-BOTTOM
FRAME

75

150

THREADED PINS WELDED TO
STEEL PLATE PRIOR TO
GALVANIZING

STEEL COVER PLATE PAINT
FINISH

DETAIL 1

BOTTOM FRAME

5

6

4   Entry lobby initial plan sketch
5   Entry canopy detail
6   Entrance canopy
Photography: courtesy Rihs Architects

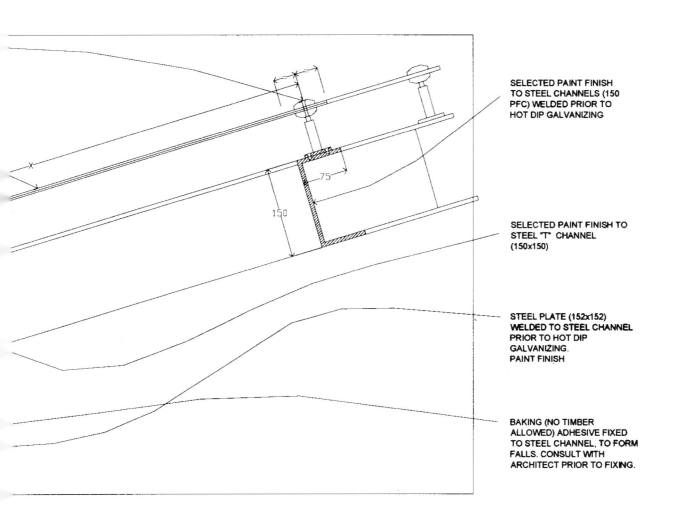

SELECTED PAINT FINISH
TO STEEL CHANNELS (150
PFC) WELDED PRIOR TO
HOT DIP GALVANIZING

SELECTED PAINT FINISH TO
STEEL "T" CHANNEL
(150x150)

STEEL PLATE (152x152)
WELDED TO STEEL CHANNEL
PRIOR TO HOT DIP
GALVANIZING.
PAINT FINISH

BAKING (NO TIMBER
ALLOWED) ADHESIVE FIXED
TO STEEL CHANNEL, TO FORM
FALLS. CONSULT WITH
ARCHITECT PRIOR TO FIXING.

MULTI-LEVEL CEILINGS AND BULKHEADS

RESIDENCE, DOUBLE BAY, NEW SOUTH WALES, AUSTRALIA

Rihs Architects

1&2   Ceiling details
3   Lightwell/kitchen bulkhead
4&5   Floor plans
6   Section
7   Stairwell ceiling edge detail

Rigorous constraints imposed by a tight building envelope within a similarly constrained site required innovative ways of overcoming changes in level and specific services reticulation. The architect also required a column-free structure despite some highly unusual loads for a single residence.

The traditional methods of a combination of ceilings and bulkheads was not going to be up to the high standards of finishing and details achieved elsewhere. A more open and innovative solution was needed.

The introduction of true layered ceilings connected to each other through the use of recessed vertical bulkheads and combined with each layer having a sharply tapered end at each visible ceiling edge provided the lightness and sharpness of details consistent with the design details of the remainder of the residence.

Ceilings and bulkheads could then become additional sculptural elements either complementing or adding to the dynamism of the design by providing accents of light or shadow at day or night time.

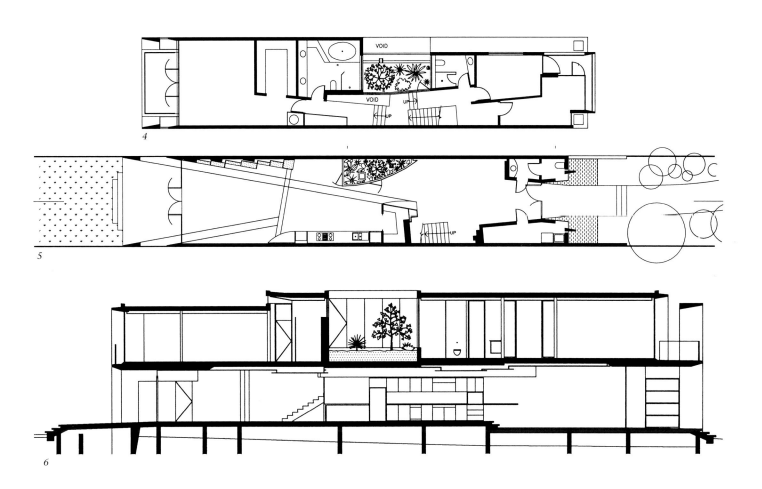

4

5

6

7

8

Photography: Simon Kenny (1,3,8); courtesy Rihs Architects

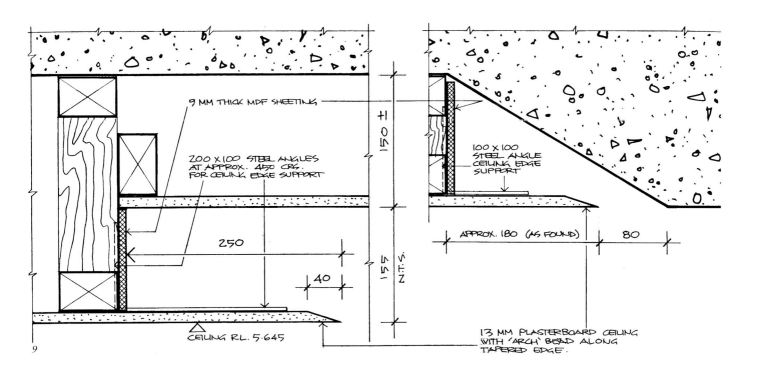

9 MM THICK MDF SHEETING

200 X 100 STEEL ANGLES AT APPROX. 450 CRS. FOR CEILING EDGE SUPPORT

150 ±

250

155 N.T.S.

40

CEILING R.L. 5.645

9

100 X 100 STEEL ANGLE CEILING EDGE SUPPORT

APPROX. 180 (AS FOUND)   80

13 MM PLASTERBOARD CEILING WITH 'ARCH' BEAD ALONG TAPERED EDGE.

10

RIBBED INTERIOR WOODEN WALL
BRIEFING CENTER, SILICON GRAPHICS, MOUNTAIN VIEW, CALIFORNIA, USA
STUDIOS Architecture

1

1 Lantern-like Reality Center conveys sense
   of contained energy
2 Detail of steel, wood and flourescent-lit
   ribs enclosing theatre
3 Floor plan

The client makes both computer hardware and software used for extremely sophisticated applications, such as 3D modelling, weather simulations and total immersion theatre.

The Briefing Center, part of a corporate campus also designed by STUDIOS Architecture, is used for sales and marketing. Equipped with conference rooms and demonstration areas, the centre sits at the main entry to the SGI campus. It consists of two wings running behind and away from the main lobby and reception area.

A fulcrum plan for the centre was devised to unify the space, with the pivot between the two angled wings defined by differing floor materials and a hanging, circular stainless steel valance.

One path dead-ends at the theatre, a multi-sensory cinema designed by STUDIOS to showcase SGI components and applications.

Taking strategies used in exhibit design, the centre's fulcrum plan places a series of conference and screening rooms around a luminous high bay space leading the visitor into a widening program of experiences.

2

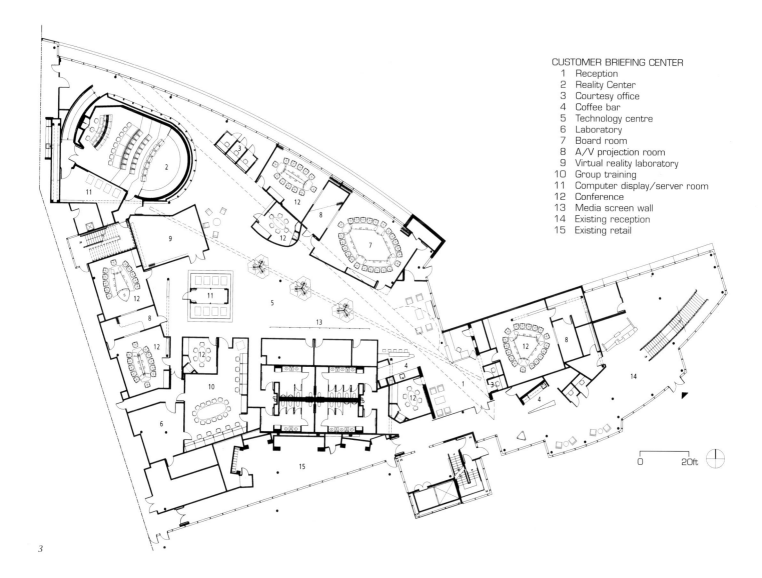

CUSTOMER BRIEFING CENTER
1 Reception
2 Reality Center
3 Courtesy office
4 Coffee bar
5 Technology centre
6 Laboratory
7 Board room
8 A/V projection room
9 Virtual reality laboratory
10 Group training
11 Computer display/server room
12 Conference
13 Media screen wall
14 Existing reception
15 Existing retail

0 20ft

3

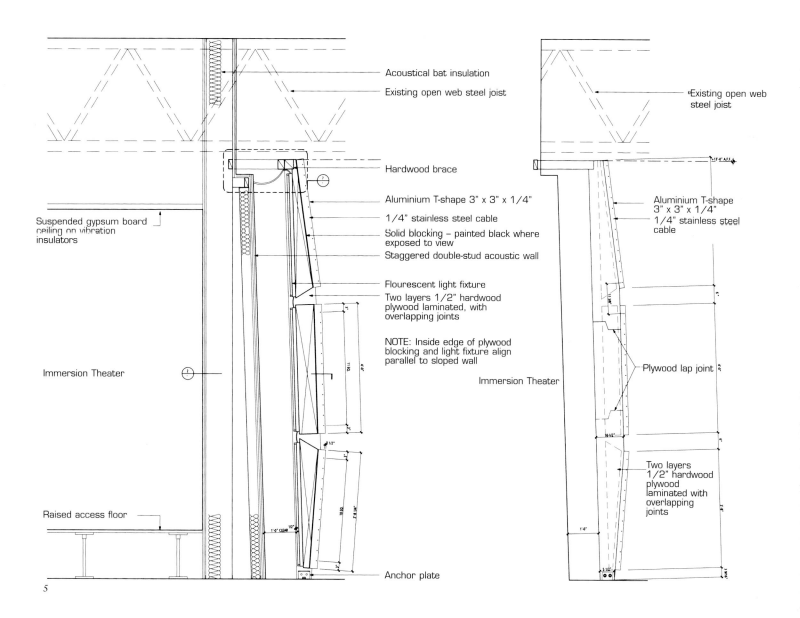

Acoustical bat insulation

Existing open web steel joist

Existing open web steel joist

Hardwood brace

Aluminium T-shape 3" x 3" x 1/4"

1/4" stainless steel cable

Solid blocking – painted black where exposed to view

Staggered double-stud acoustic wall

Flourescent light fixture

Two layers 1/2" hardwood plywood laminated, with overlapping joints

NOTE: Inside edge of plywood blocking and light fixture align parallel to sloped wall

Aluminium T-shape 3" x 3" x 1/4"

1/4" stainless steel cable

Plywood lap joint

Two layers 1/2" hardwood plywood laminated with overlapping joints

Suspended gypsum board ceiling on vibration insulators

Immersion Theater

Immersion Theater

Raised access floor

Anchor plate

5

From the greeting area and lounge, one is drawn by carefully sequenced spaces, past working hardware which is exhibited on an understated wooden podium, and through an array of self-directed displays, towards the Reality Center.

The face of the theatre is burnt orange with a shell of maple lighting ribs. Lantern-like in appearance, it conveys a sense of contained energy, like a super-scaled component of the image-making machinery it holds.

Pale green limestone and dark grey slate, maple, stainless steel, and plate glass that refracts both moss green and copper hues, mark the customer spaces through understated color and texture.

Opposite:
Interiors of Reality Center Immersion Theater
5 *Reality Center wall section*

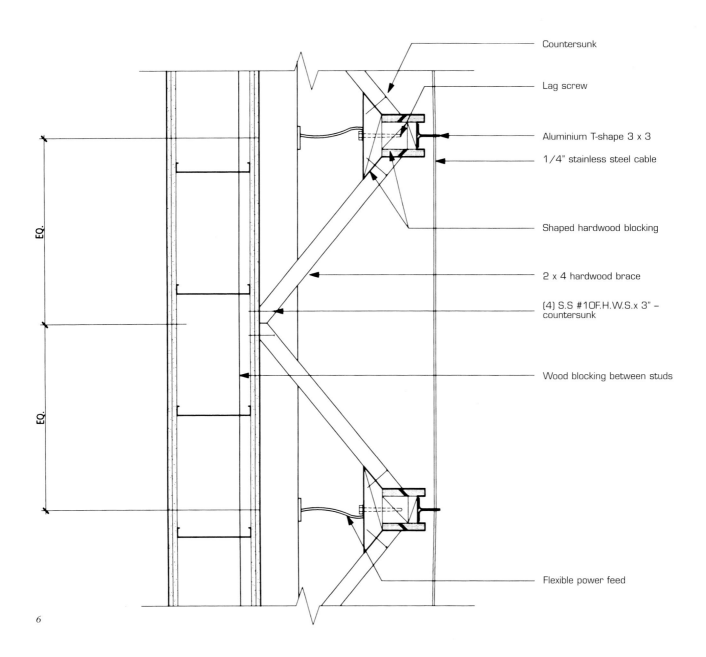

Countersunk

Lag screw

Aluminium T-shape 3 x 3

1/4" stainless steel cable

Shaped hardwood blocking

2 x 4 hardwood brace

(4) S.S #10F.H.W.S.x 3" –
countersunk

Wood blocking between studs

Flexible power feed

EQ.

EQ.

6

6–8   Reality Center rib details
Photography: Michael O'Callahan

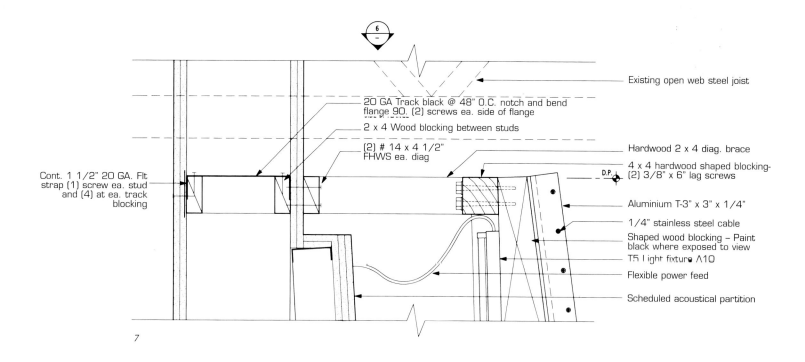

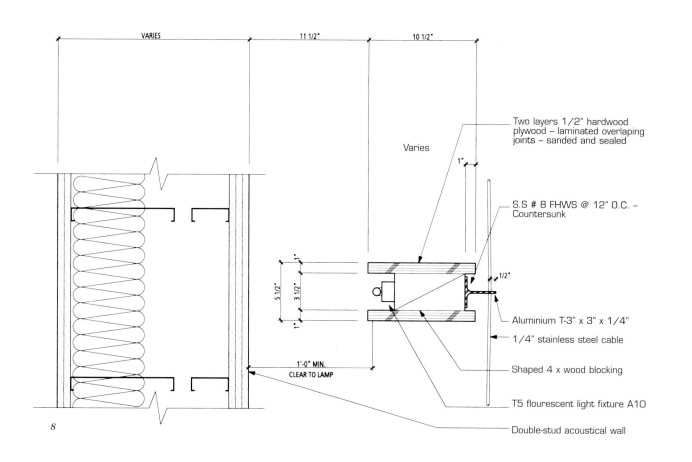

Existing open web steel joist

20 GA Track black @ 48" O.C. notch and bend flange 90. (2) screws ea. side of flange

2 x 4 Wood blocking between studs

(2) # 14 x 4 1/2" FHWS ea. diag

Hardwood 2 x 4 diag. brace

4 x 4 hardwood shaped blocking- (2) 3/8" x 6" lag screws

Aluminium T-3" x 3" x 1/4"

1/4" stainless steel cable

Shaped wood blocking – Paint black where exposed to view

T5 light fixture A10

Flexible power feed

Scheduled acoustical partition

Cont. 1 1/2" 20 GA. Flt strap (1) screw ea. stud and (4) at ea. track blocking

D.P.

7

VARIES   11 1/2"   10 1/2"

Varies

Two layers 1/2" hardwood plywood – laminated overlaping joints – sanded and sealed

1"

S.S # 8 FHWS @ 12" O.C. – Countersunk

1/2"

5 1/2"   3 1/2"

1"

1"

Aluminium T-3" x 3" x 1/4"

1/4" stainless steel cable

Shaped 4 x wood blocking

T5 flourescent light fixture A10

1'-0" MIN.
CLEAR TO LAMP

Double-stud acoustical wall

8

SKYLIGHT, GLAZED WALLS, MESH SCREENS AND SUNSHADES
QUEENSWAY SECONDARY SCHOOL, MINISTRY OF EDUCATION, REPUBLIC OF SINGAPORE
TSP Architects + Planners Pte Ltd

1

1   *Detail of toppling 'canister' and corridor screening*
2   *East elevation of first and second volume*
3   *Site plan*

The new additions were built over the old school site founded in 1961. Within such a constricted lot, the close contact between the various entities manifested into three distinct volumes, each juxtaposed in a mass of colliding and tilting planes.

Such gesture is profound in the first volume that features a toppling 'canister' to echo the mode of oppression. The act has given rise to a double-volume library lit by glazed roof planes that connect a glazed wall to form a continuous bent plane of glass. The structure is comprised primarily of hollow steel sections with snap-on capping to hold the glazing in place.

The second volume of six-storey sections offers human circulation contained behind a huge screen of mesh to form a translucent barrier between the users and the surrounding community. It gives a soft texture to the concrete structure surface form.

The third volume of four-storey sections is protected by a series of climatic responsive shades. A calculated projection of 2.6 metres of shade helps to cast a long shadow over and beyond the fenestrations. Similar shades protect the highly exposed façade of the second volume fronting an open field, which minimises the heat transmission through the wall of fabric as well as through the glazed openings.

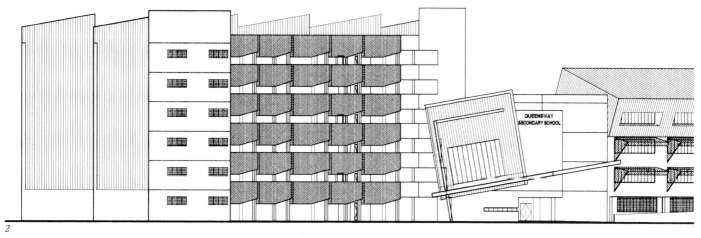

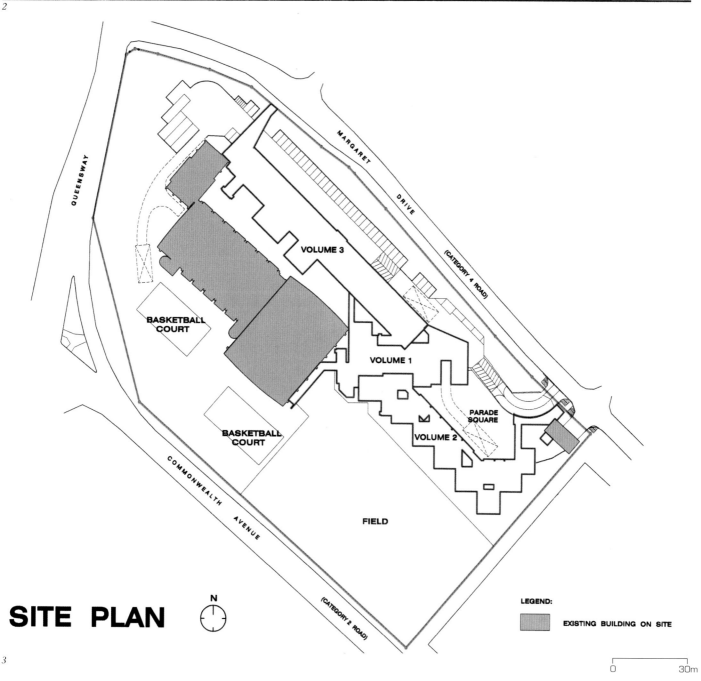

QUEENSWAY
SECONDARY SCHOOL

VOLUME 3

VOLUME 1

PARADE
SQUARE

VOLUME 2

BASKETBALL
COURT

BASKETBALL
COURT

FIELD

QUEENSWAY

MARGARET DRIVE

(CATEGORY 4 ROAD)

COMMONWEALTH AVENUE

(CATEGORY 2 ROAD)

SITE PLAN

N

LEGEND:

EXISTING BUILDING ON SITE

0   30m

4

5

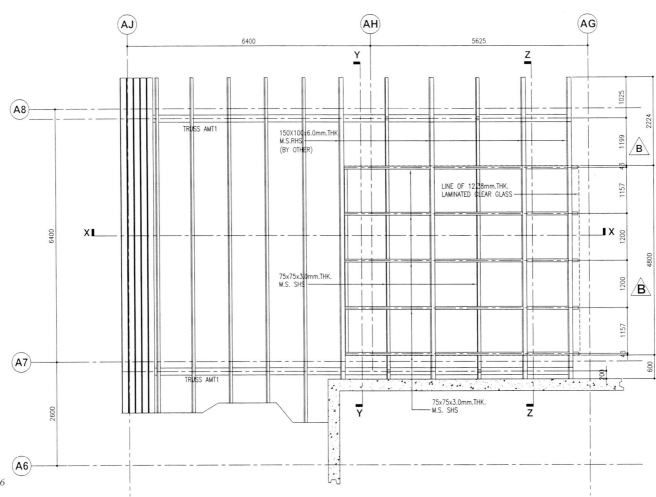

6

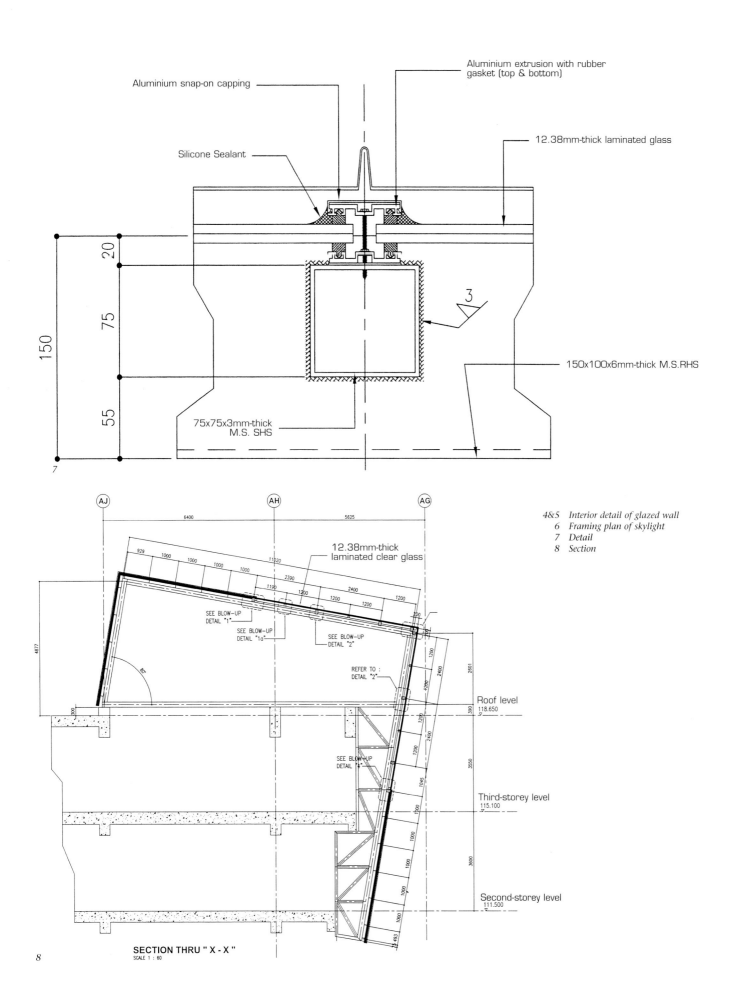

Aluminium snap-on capping

Aluminium extrusion with rubber
gasket (top & bottom)

Silicone Sealant

12.38mm-thick laminated glass

150x100x6mm-thick M.S.RHS

20

75

150

55

3

75x75x3mm-thick
M.S. SHS

7

4&5   Interior detail of glazed wall
6   Framing plan of skylight
7   Detail
8   Section

AJ   AH   AG

6400   5625

929   1000   1000   1000   1000   11020

12.38mm-thick
laminated clear glass

2390

1190   1200   1200   2400   1200

SEE BLOW-UP
DETAIL "1"

SEE BLOW-UP
DETAIL "1a"

SEE BLOW-UP
DETAIL "2"

4877

87

REFER TO :
DETAIL "2"

1200

2400

2601

1200

Roof level
118.650

390

SEE BLOW-UP
DETAIL "3"

1200

2400

1045

3550

Third-storey level
115.100

1000

1200

1000

3600

Second-storey level
111.500

1000

8

SECTION THRU " X - X "
SCALE 1 : 60

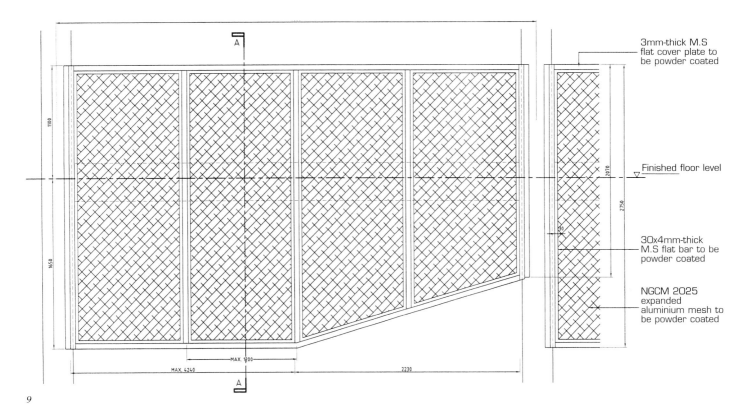

3mm-thick M.S
flat cover plate to
be powder coated

Finished floor level

30x4mm-thick
M.S flat bar to be
powder coated

NGCM 2025
expanded
aluminium mesh to
be powder coated

9

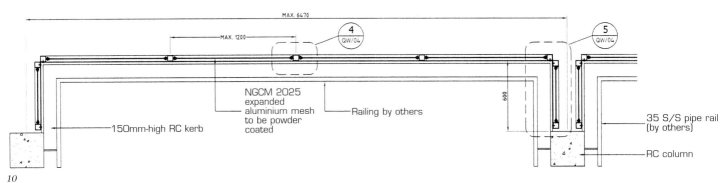

MAX. 6470

MAX. 1200

4
QW/04

5
QW/04

NGCM 2025
expanded
aluminium mesh
to be powder
coated

Railing by others

150mm-high RC kerb

600

35 S/S pipe rail
(by others)

RC column

10

11

9   Typical elevation of sunshade
10   Section of sunshade
11&13 Detail of corridor screens
12   Detail of sunshade
14   Detail of steel framing and expanded mesh

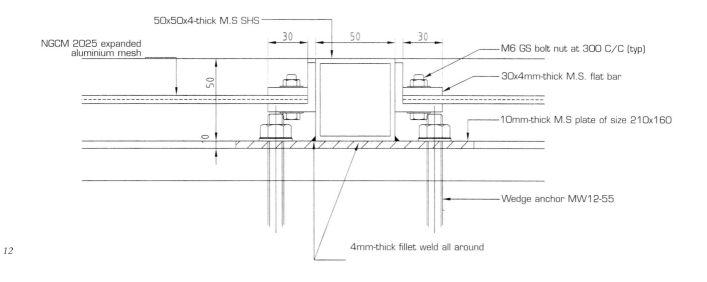

50x50x4-thick M.S SHS

NGCM 2025 expanded aluminium mesh

30

50

30

M6 GS bolt nut at 300 C/C (typ)

30x4mm-thick M.S. flat bar

50

10mm-thick M.S plate of size 210x160

Wedge anchor MW12-55

4mm-thick fillet weld all around

12

13

14

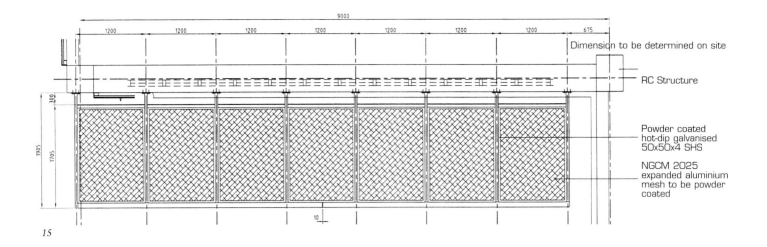

9000

1200 1200 1200 1200 1200 1200 1200 675

Dimension to be determined on site

RC Structure

1905 1705 300

Powder coated
hot-dip galvanised
50x50x4 SHS

NGCM 2025
expanded aluminium
mesh to be powder
coated

10

15

16

17

15 *Plan of mesh sunshade*
16 *Detail of sunshades*
17 *Detail of aluminium cladding with
    sunshades*
18 *Side elevation of sunshades*
19 *Elevation of sunshades*

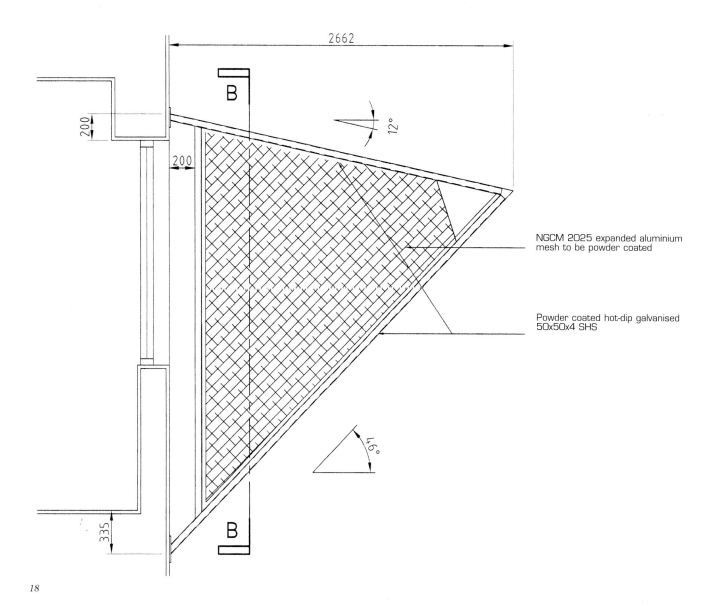

2662

200

200

12°

B

B

335

46°

NGCM 2025 expanded aluminium
mesh to be powder coated

Powder coated hot-dip galvanised
50x50x4 SHS

18

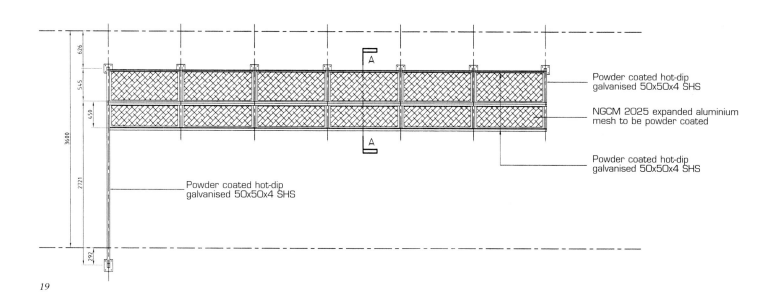

626

545

450

3600

2721

292

A

A

Powder coated hot-dip
galvanised 50x50x4 SHS

NGCM 2025 expanded aluminium
mesh to be powder coated

Powder coated hot-dip
galvanised 50x50x4 SHS

Powder coated hot-dip
galvanised 50x50x4 SHS

19

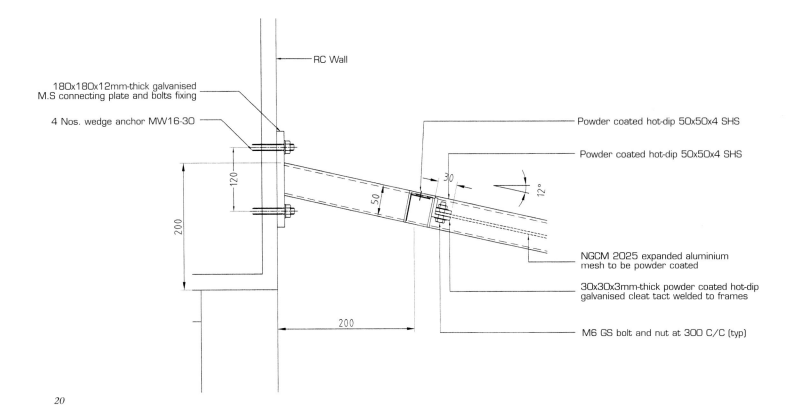

RC Wall

180x180x12mm-thick galvanised
M.S connecting plate and bolts fixing

4 Nos. wedge anchor MW16-30

Powder coated hot-dip 50x50x4 SHS

Powder coated hot-dip 50x50x4 SHS

120

200

50

30

12°

NGCM 2025 expanded aluminium
mesh to be powder coated

30x30x3mm-thick powder coated hot-dip
galvanised cleat tact welded to frames

200

M6 GS bolt and nut at 300 C/C (typ)

20

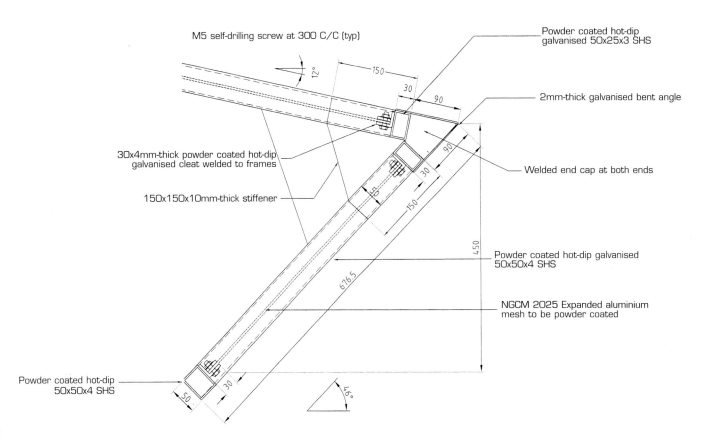

M5 self-drilling screw at 300 C/C (typ)

Powder coated hot-dip
galvanised 50x25x3 SHS

12°

150

30

90

2mm-thick galvanised bent angle

30x4mm-thick powder coated hot-dip
galvanised cleat welded to frames

150x150x10mm-thick stiffener

90

30

Welded end cap at both ends

150

450

676.5

Powder coated hot-dip galvanised
50x50x4 SHS

NGCM 2025 Expanded aluminium
mesh to be powder coated

Powder coated hot-dip
50x50x4 SHS

50

30

46°

21

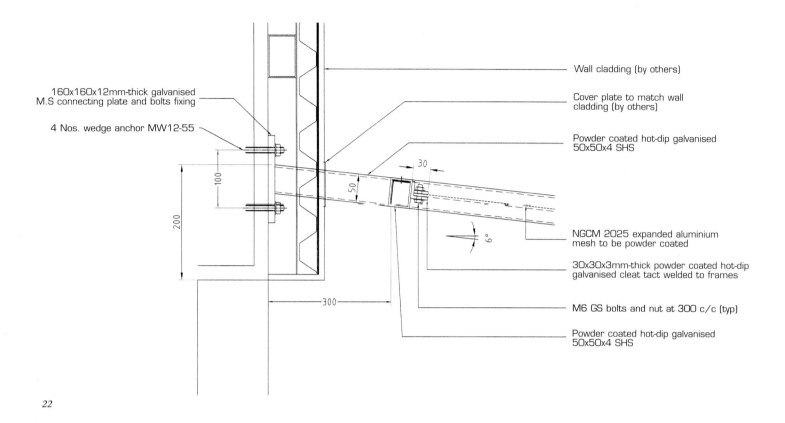

160x160x12mm-thick galvanised
M.S connecting plate and bolts fixing

4 Nos. wedge anchor MW12-55

Wall cladding (by others)

Cover plate to match wall
cladding (by others)

Powder coated hot-dip galvanised
50x50x4 SHS

NGCM 2025 expanded aluminium
mesh to be powder coated

30x30x3mm-thick powder coated hot-dip
galvanised cleat tact welded to frames

M6 GS bolts and nut at 300 c/c (typ)

Powder coated hot-dip galvanised
50x50x4 SHS

22

23

24

20&21 Detail of sunshades
22 Section of mesh shades
23 Detail of sunshades on four-storey
block
24 Night scene revealing glazed walls
and screens
Photography: Albert KS Lim (23,24);
Lawrence PC Tan (1,4,5,11,13,14,16,17)

WALL PANELS
WHITE CHAPEL, ROSE-HULMAN INSTITUTE OF TECHNOLOGY, TERRE HAUTE, INDIANA, USA
VOA Associates Incorporated Architecture / Planning / Interior Design

1

1   *South elevation with outdoor terrace*
2   *Building section*

The White Chapel is a non-denominational place of worship located on the campus of the highly regarded Rose-Hulman Institute of Technology. It fulfils a long-term goal of creating a special place where the campus can gather in worship and where individual counselling can take place.

The 500-square-metre chapel consists of a wedge-shaped nave supported by an entry narthex, counselling offices, service pantry, toilets and mechanical spaces. The nave is a semi-conical shell defined by a series of steel tube arches, which increase in size from the back of the nave to the front. Diamond-shaped, stainless steel panels clad the exterior of the nave shell. The shell is split by a series of vertical ribbon windows and a

continuous ridge skylight. The entire east end of the nave is glazed so that the campus creates a backdrop for activities within the chapel.

A long, curved limestone wall bisects the nave and extends out into the site. Visitors approaching the chapel follow a path along this wall to the entrance. An outdoor garden terrace creates a forecourt to the chapel.

A waterfall and water channel define the southern edge of the terrace, creating a boundary between the everyday world and this place for contemplation and celebration, one that speaks to the spirit as well as the mind.

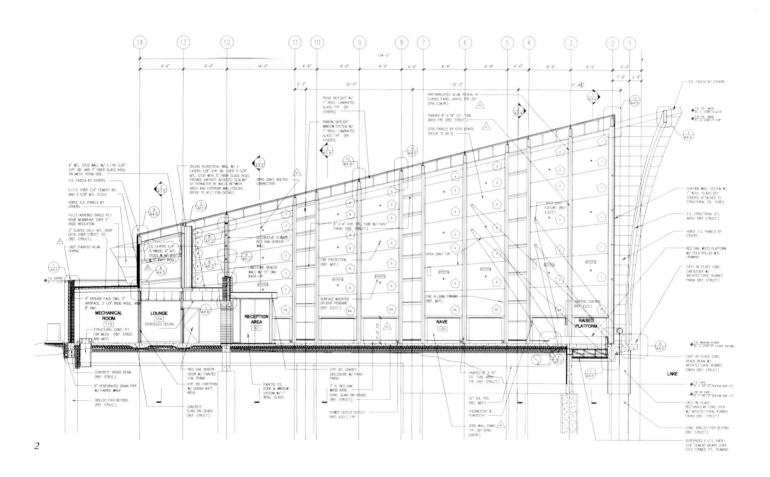

2

The essence of the chapel is structure and enclosure, defining the main worship space as a single simple yet dynamic volume. The design sought to reduce elements of structure and enclosure to their most basic components, eliminating anything that was superfluous or redundant.

In this search for elemental simplicity, the geometry of the building drove almost every decision, from the selection of the structural and building enclosure system to the detailing of the mechanical, electrical and fire protection system and the design of the room acoustics.

4

Opposite:
Chapel interior with steel tube arches and acoustic panels
4   *Lake view of chapel*
5   *Elevation of nave*

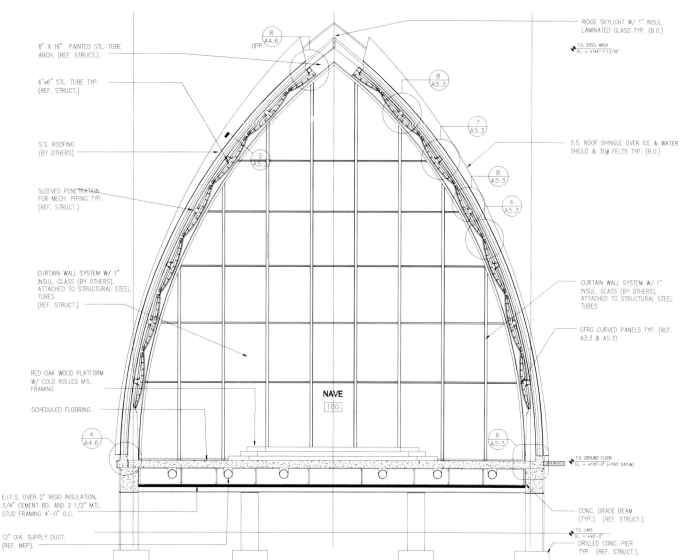

8" X 16" PAINTED STL. TUBE ARCH. (REF. STRUCT.).

6"x6" STL. TUBE TYP. (REF. STRUCT.)

S.S. ROOFING (BY OTHERS)

SLEEVED PENETRATION FOR MECH. PIPING TYP. (REF. STRUCT.)

CURTAIN WALL SYSTEM W/ 1" INSUL. GLASS (BY OTHERS), ATTACHED TO STRUCTURAL STEEL TUBES (REF. STRUCT.)

RED OAK WOOD PLATFORM W/ COLD ROLLED MTL. FRAMING

SCHEDULED FLOORING.

E.I.F.S. OVER 2" RIGID INSULATION, 3/4" CEMENT BD. AND 2 1/2" MTL. STUD FRAMING 4'-0" O.C.

12" DIA. SUPPLY DUCT. (REF. MEP).

RIDGE SKYLIGHT W/ 1" INSUL. LAMINATED GLASS TYP. (B.O.)

T.O. STEEL ARCH
EL. = +145'-7 13/16"

S.S. ROOF SHINGLE OVER ICE & WATER SHEILD & 30# FELTS TYP. (B.O.)

CURTAIN WALL SYSTEM W/ 1" INSUL. GLASS (BY OTHERS), ATTACHED TO STRUCTURAL STEEL TUBES

GFRG CURVED PANELS TYP. (REF. A3.3 & A5.3)

NAVE
100

T.O. GROUND FLOOR
EL. = +100'-0" (+550' DATUM)

CONC. GRADE BEAM (TYP.). (REF. STRUCT.).

T.O. LAKE
EL. = +92'-0"

DRILLED CONC. PIER TYP. (REF. STRUCT.).

5

As is fitting for an engineering school, the expression of structure and the precision in detailing building systems were underlying principles in the building design. The design mission was to instruct as well as delight.

The chapel is supported on a foundation of caissons and concrete grade beams. Four of these caissons, which support the front of the chapel, were drilled in the lake bottom, requiring the construction of a temporary cofferdam.

The principal structure is a series of 14 rectangular steel tube arches, rolled into a Gothic profile. No two arches are alike. Connecting the arches horizontally are square steel tubes set so that they intersect the arches in a consistent radial pattern. Rectangular steel tubes provide the support structure for the eastern curtainwall.

The exterior is clad in interlocking diamond-shaped stainless steel panels applied over an ice-and-water shield membrane over NRG insulation board attached to a corrugated metal deck. The deck is attached to the steel tube arches.

Access to the site was restricted on three sides, requiring the use of cranes and 25-metre lifts to erect the structure and exterior cladding. The ribbon windows and ridge skylight are butt glazed and were installed integrally with the stainless steel cladding.

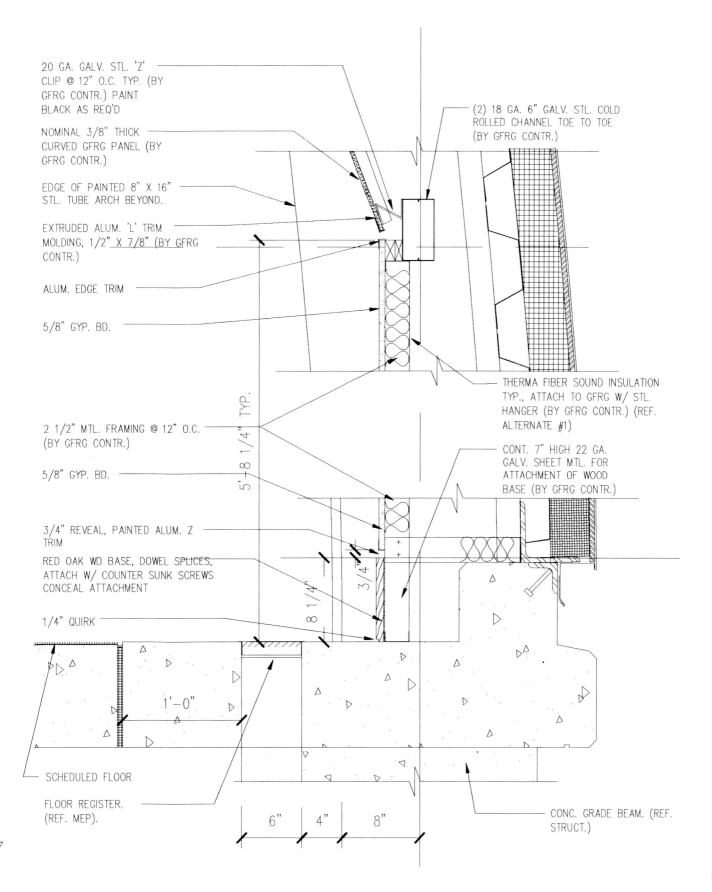

20 GA. GALV. STL. 'Z' CLIP @ 12" O.C. TYP. (BY GFRG CONTR.) PAINT BLACK AS REQ'D

NOMINAL 3/8" THICK CURVED GFRG PANEL (BY GFRG CONTR.)

EDGE OF PAINTED 8" X 16" STL. TUBE ARCH BEYOND.

EXTRUDED ALUM. 'L' TRIM MOLDING, 1/2" X 7/8" (BY GFRG CONTR.)

ALUM. EDGE TRIM

5/8" GYP. BD.

2 1/2" MTL. FRAMING @ 12" O.C. (BY GFRG CONTR.)

5/8" GYP. BD.

3/4" REVEAL, PAINTED ALUM. Z TRIM

RED OAK WD BASE, DOWEL SPLICES, ATTACH W/ COUNTER SUNK SCREWS CONCEAL ATTACHMENT

1/4" QUIRK

SCHEDULED FLOOR

FLOOR REGISTER. (REF. MEP).

(2) 18 GA. 6" GALV. STL. COLD ROLLED CHANNEL TOE TO TOE (BY GFRG CONTR.)

THERMA FIBER SOUND INSULATION TYP., ATTACH TO GFRG W/ STL. HANGER (BY GFRG CONTR.) (REF. ALTERNATE #1)

CONT. 7" HIGH 22 GA. GALV. SHEET MTL. FOR ATTACHMENT OF WOOD BASE (BY GFRG CONTR.)

CONC. GRADE BEAM. (REF. STRUCT.)

5'-8 1/4" TYP.

8 1/4"

3/4"

1'-0"

6" 4" 8"

7

INDEX

ACKNOWLEDGMENTS

IMAGES is pleased to add *Details in Architecture, Creative Detailing by Some of the World's Leading Architects, Volume 4* to its compendium of design and architectural publications.

We wish to thank all participating firms for their valuable contribution to this publication.

In particular, we would like to thank Foster and Partners for allowing the use of their photograph and plans on the cover and divider pages of this book.

We are also most grateful to Mark McInturff of McInturff Architects, for writing the Foreword for this book.